D1622387

Design for Happiness

William V. Myres

Design

FOR

Happiness

BROADMAN PRESS
Nashville, Tennessee

Library of Congress catalog card number: 61–12416

Printed in the United States of America

5.MH61K.S.P.

To those who have taught me most—
my parents, my family, my students

Preface

ALMOST EVERYONE has—or thinks he has—at least one book he must write. This is mine.

If he is a teacher, students gratify his ego by asking, "Why don't you put your ideas in a book?" Later on, others may ask, "Why did you?"

But why another book on the Sermon on the Mount?

I have felt for some time there is a place for a purely psychological interpretation of the Sermon on the Mount. It is my belief that a problem-solving psychological emphasis was the Sermon's original setting.

I have tried to bridge the gap between first-century language and twentieth-century psychological terms. The ideas are not different, just the words. To me, one thing stands out above all else—Jesus had no peer on any subject on which he spoke. There is only one Jesus.

It would be impossible to thank individually all who have contributed to this book. But my indebtedness remains.

WILLIAM VENTING MYRES

Contents

1

You Can Be Happy

YOU CAN BE happy. Jesus said so, and he meant it. Twenty centuries of time have failed to disprove his plan for happiness and contentment. As a matter of fact, time has proved Jesus was correct. Jesus' teachings for a happy, stable, adjusted life are reflected in much present-day psychology and psychiatry. His principles are being advocated today as though men have discovered something new.

Strangely enough, a great many people think that the' psychology of personal adjustment is a twentieth-century development. The terms used are rather new, but the psychological principles involved are as old as humanity itself. For hundreds and hundreds of years the Bible has been calling attention to psychological principles to make life more livable.

Time has failed to improve upon the fundamental psychological conditions advocated by the man from Nazareth. No, the current terms are not found in the Bible, but the psychological principles of personal adjustment are there in abundance. The Gospel writer John could hardly have been more correct when he said of Jesus that he "needed no one to bear witness of man; for he himself knew what was in man."

Yes, Jesus knew the secret of a happy, stable, contented life. And the very things he taught are being used by psychiatrists and psychologists today. The principles are the same; only the names have been changed to confuse the ignorant.

The substance of Jesus' plan for happiness and security is found in the Sermon on the Mount, as recorded in Matthew's Gospel. Strangely enough, the many interpretations of this body of Jesus' teachings have obscured its meaning about the happiness, contentment, adjustment, and security which made Jesus the most completely adjusted person who has ever lived.

Study in Confusion

Unfortunately, the psychological emphases of Jesus were discarded by the religionists in favor of some theological emphasis. It has been due largely to the efforts of the students of psychology that the psychological emphases of Jesus in the Sermon on the Mount have been recovered. They have pointed out that Jesus was trying to teach people how to live better with themselves, with others, and with God.

Confusion is at once apparent when the various efforts of men to interpret the Sermon on the Mount are considered. Historically, there have been a number of interpretative approaches. And while the Sermon on the Mount is primarily psychological, this real emphasis has been recovered only in recent years.

By and large, some otherworldly emphasis has found expression in several interesting theories. But these theories have served to hide the psychological emphases which Jesus made primary.

One such theory is the so-called postponed kingdom approach. Those who hold to this basis of interpretation insist that it was Jesus' intention to set up his kingdom on earth.

And the teachings in the Sermon on the Mount were to be the kingdom laws or rules. However, since men rejected him, the kingdom is postponed until his second coming. When Jesus does return, these are to be his rules for governing an earthly kingdom then. This approach makes the Sermon on the Mount entirely futuristic in application. It completely sets aside the inescapable emphasis Jesus made for immediate living.

Another theory advocated by many has been called the pagan approach. This theory holds that the Sermon is too idealistic for a practical man. Therefore, no one is expected to practice the teachings in daily living. It is evident the great rank and file of the masses follow some ill-defined idea that the teachings are wonderfully ethical, but that they are too idealistic for practical living. Such statements as "religion and business don't mix" lay stress to this philosophy. Many people would relegate the Sermon on the Mount to Sunday and forget it the rest of the week. This is paganistic.

A third theory has been called the literalist approach. Those who interpret the Sermon on the Mount based on such an idea say that it is to be understood as absolutely literal; i.e., when Jesus said, "If thy right eye offend thee pluck it out," he meant just that. This approach makes the Sermon a type of "hip pocket" rulebook to regulate conduct —especially the conduct of others. Such an application generally disregards plain contextual meanings and renders important teachings utterly meaningless and contradictory.

A close analysis shows that the Sermon on the Mount reveals a principles-for-living approach. It discloses principles to make life more livable. The Sermon is not a "hip pocket" rulebook to apply to the other fellow. It is not an idealistic, unworkable philosophy. It is not an emphasis for the sweet by-and-by, but rather for the difficult and perplexing now.

The most logical approach to the Sermon on the Mount is one that regards the teaching as a basis for solving personal problems. Such an understanding interprets Jesus as seeking to help people to understand themselves. Most of the teaching deals with vital problems which confront people in their day-to-day contacts and relationships. The primary emphasis is in the area of practical living and problem-solving. Whatever otherworldly emphasis the teaching may contain, it is certainly secondary to the immediate solution of personal problems.

The Sermon on the Mount, with its primary emphasis on practical living, emphasizes those aspects of personal adjustment to life situations which will minimize one's personal problems. It is therefore a practical commentary on mental hygiene.

Neurosis Is Self-made

Neurosis is the term currently applied to much unhappiness, maladjustment, and discontent. Someone has said that the difference between a neurotic and a psychotic is that the psychotic thinks two plus two equals five while the neurotic knows two plus two equals four but lets this knowledge worry him.

From a nontechnical point of view, neurosis is the continuance of personal maladjustment. It lasts long after there is no objective reason for the problem to continue. And a neurosis often results from selecting some childish response when the problem first arises.

Why should a person be terrified as he thinks about a previous experience? There is no objective stimulus present to create any real danger. Yet, the danger seems very real to the one who is mentally reliving the experience. Likely, his primary problem is that he did not make a mature adjustment to his difficulty when it first arose. But, if he is ever to be released from his fear, he must make a mature adjustment. Sometimes the release comes from learning what the real problem is and then facing that problem squarely. He may find that what he thought was his problem is merely a symptom of childish, selfish living.

The neurosis, which causes the so-called nervous breakdown, arises because people refuse, or fail, to live unselfishly. They refuse to grow up psychologically, choosing rather to live like children. Biological maturity bears no absolute relationship to psychological maturity.

A happy, stable, secure, adjusted person is the product of one's attitudes toward life, people, and property. Happiness or unhappiness is self-made. Adjustment or neurosis is determined by each person for himself. No one nor anything within itself can cause another to have a nervous breakdown. Such trouble can come only by the adverse way in which the individual interprets and reacts to a situation.

Again, one's attitudes determine his likes and dislikes. How else can one understand that Mary is liked by Sue but not by Martha? Mary is essentially the same girl. But Martha has made a decision not to like Mary, while Sue has made a decision to like her. Basically, it is the attitude of the one who likes or dislikes which makes the difference. The same principle which applies to people also applies to things. Otherwise, we would all like the same people and things and dislike the same people and things.

Life is largely what one makes it. True, there are certain bounds within which each life develops. But within these bounds, a person's outlook has much to do with the kind of life he lives. Within these limits he makes various choices. These either help or hinder his having a happy, secure life. These may be conscious choices or they may be unconscious, coming from habits previously developed. Sometimes one chooses not to choose. Yet, this within itself is an actual choice. And each and every choice has some effect which tends to make life more or less livable.

The Sermon on the Mount treats the vital relationships of a man with himself, with his fellow man, and with his God. As such, it becomes a design for happiness. The teachings contain the substance of the abundant life. Men are confused in their ideas as to what constitutes the good life. Many think it consists of doing things and having things. When Jesus said to the rich young ruler, "If thou wilt enter into life," he was talking to a young man who thought himself already very much alive. But Jesus realized that there was a problem which defeated his actually entering into life. The young man himself recognized that there was something missing in his life which kept him from being happy. He came to Jesus unhappy and went away unhappy, for he was unwilling to do what Jesus told him would make for his happiness.

Psychological problems are due mainly to faulty adjustments to reality. After all, real living is primarily a spiritual matter. The Sermon on the Mount reveals all of the areas of necessary adjustment in life—those which constitute the vital problems of living. It also discloses forces that stimulate problems for people and points out how one may avoid unnecessary problems in the matters of day-to-day living.

The Sermon on the Mount is essentially a design for real living. As such, it offers one the opportunity to study those areas of his life which make him either happy or unhappy, stable or unstable, secure or insecure.

2

Examine Your Personal Attitudes

And seeing the multitudes, he went up into the mountain: and when he had sat down, his disciples came unto him: and he opened his mouth and taught them, saying,

Blessed are the poor in spirit: for theirs is the kingdom of heaven.

Blessed are they that mourn: for they shall be comforted.

Blessed are the meek: for they shall inherit the earth.

Blessed are they that hunger and thirst after righteousness: for they shall be filled.

Blessed are the merciful: for they shall obtain mercy.

Blessed are the pure in heart: for they shall see God.

Blessed are the peacemakers: for they shall be called sons of God.

Blessed are they that have been persecuted for righteousness' sake: for theirs is the kingdom of heaven. Blessed are ye when men shall reproach you, and persecute you, and say all manner of evil against you falsely, for my sake. Rejoice, and be exceeding glad: for great is your reward in heaven: for so persecuted they the prophets that were before you.

Ye are the salt of the earth: but if the salt have lost its savor, wherewith shall it be salted? it is thenceforth good for nothing, but to be cast out and trodden under foot of men. Ye are the light of the world. A city set on a hill cannot be hid. Neither do men light a lamp, and put it under the bushel, but on the stand; and it shineth unto all that are in the house. Even so let your light shine before men; that they may see your good works, and glorify your Father who is in heaven (Matt. 5:1–16, ASV).

THE BEATITUDES offer Jesus' bases of personal adjustment. Jesus emphasized those characteristics in human personality which make for strong, stable personalities. The individual is viewed from his own standpoint. Someone has well said that we may escape from everyone except ourselves. No matter where we go, we are there. The fact that we have to live with ourselves frequently becomes one of our most difficult problems. The Associated Press carried a dispatch several years ago of the suicide of a noted newspaper columnist. A note at his side revealed the reason for his action: he was tired of making up excuses for living each succeeding twenty-four hours.

The Beatitudes contain statements of the points where a person is most open to attack. A violation of these points leads to personality disintegration. An affirmative response leads to personality health, or, as in vogue today, mental hygiene. Jesus was a mental hygienist without rival.

The key word of the beatitudes is translated "blessed" or "happy." Many people have regarded this word as a pious or holy word. They have failed, therefore, to understand its psychological import. Actually, the word in the original language contains the idea of a stable, adjusted, happy, secure person. Unfortunately, the English word "happy" in its present-day meaning is too meager to do justice to the concept. The original Greek word was used largely regarding outward prosperity. Homer and Pindar applied it to the gods and also to men. The Septuagint usage of it implied moral quality.

As used in the context, the word "blessed" will not lend itself to an interpretation that has connection with outward prosperity, since the very opposite is apparent. This is one of the words which has been transformed through its New

Testament usage. It appears to have been the express purpose of Jesus to refute the contemporary notion that blessedness or happiness is tied up with outward prosperity. Jesus was dealing in the realm of the personal and inward rather than the outward.

This word translated "blessed" is the same word contained in the Septuagint to translate the concept of stable blessedness in the first Psalm. To describe this blessedness the psalmist says, "he shall be like a tree planted by rivers of water." The element of stability is revealed. As the tree that is planted by rivers of water is stable and secure, so also the one who is blessed is likewise stable and secure.

The blessed life is the stable and secure life. In the beatitudes Jesus calls attention to personal attitudes, which enable one to make the necessary adjustment for a more stable life. The matter of attitude in any situation is paramount. In the final analysis, attitude is determined by the way one looks at a situation, not by the situation itself. How else can the apparent contradiction in this couplet be explained?

> Two men looked out from jail bars.
> One saw mud, the other saw stars.

Though psychology is as ancient as man, its present-day terms are comparatively new. At least this is true of the technical meanings given to it in the past fifty years. In this word "blessed" there is contained an ancient psychological concept that needs interpretation in terms of today's psychology. The concept is not new, but today the term embracing it has a rather technical meaning. This term is "adjusted." It carries with it the notion of one who has met a problem or problems positively and has found the proper adjustment thereto. There is stability involved that comes from a personal victory over that which can cause personality breakdown. Interpreted in this light, in the first Beatitude Jesus would be saying something like this: "Adjusted or stable are the poor in spirit for theirs is the kingdom of the heavens." Likewise, ideas of personal stability, security, and adjustment are found in each Beatitude.

Minimum of Egotism

Ignorance is a relative matter. No man is exempt from it when he is out of his element. And even in his own field, there are a great many things he does not know. Thomas Edison is supposed to have said that a man is capable of grasping only one seven-millionth of the total of any idea. Though this is no doubt a general statement, it does call attention to the fact that little is really known, even by men who are supposed to know.

David was talking to his father who was a first-class mechanic. He asked his father how to extract the square root of a number.

"I don't know," said Mr. Carmon, "ask your teacher."

David replied, "Shucks, Dad, didn't you ever go to school? My teacher says even an ignoramous knows how to extract the square root."

The father, a little hurt but still patient, retorted, "Son, remember this, we're all ignorant—it's just on different subjects."

There is something very profound in the knowledge that we are all ignorant. The more one learns, the more he realizes how little he knows, even in his own field of specialization. This is the day of specialization. Men are devoting their entire time to the study of one little part of a subject. Nevertheless, no one seems to learn all there is to know about even a small fraction of a subject.

One of the great delusions of all time is to substitute names and terms for understanding. In every field of learning, a large part of it consists of mere names given to things and ideas. Each field of study has its own peculiar jargon. Often the mere giving of a name to a thing or idea is offered as a substitute for a real understanding. Too frequently the man who has learned some terminology or words not generally in use has been regarded as the educated man. Sometimes he regards himself as an intellectual. When this happens, it becomes evident that his egotism is intellectual dishonesty.

This practice of substituting names for knowledge often has a frightening effect upon one's personal stability. The more he seems successful in pawning off his words for wisdom, the more he is likely to become maladjusted and tense. He himself usually knows that he really does not know what he is talking about. He has developed a pseudo intellectual frame of mind. He feels it necessary to keep up the front. Naturally, he is going to be tense, trying to live up to the demands of such a false front. Egotism is also psychological dishonesty.

An even greater danger arises when the deluder also becomes the deluded. There are people who are accepted as an authority in a field when they are not. After a period of time they may become so convinced that they are authorities that they begin to build up within themselves the little tin god complex. In the early stages, this complex renders them maladjusted and tense. Ultimately, it may lead to more vicious personality disorders.

Jesus knew that unrestrained egotism produces self-defeat. In the Beatitude "Blessed are the poor in spirit: for theirs is the kingdom of heaven," the master psychologist sounded a fundamental principle for keeping a stable, happy, adjusted personality. Psychologically, this Beatitude means that the person who does not think too highly of himself possesses the essence of the kingdom of heaven in his personality. It is evident that, as used in this Beatitude, the kingdom of heaven does not refer primarily to a place, but to an attitude of being enriched with heavenly characteristics. Moreover, it is clear that the unegotistical people have immediate possession of this kingdom. It is not a thing which is to be received at some distant future time.

The man from Nazareth recognized the need for balance within the human ego. He taught that the temptation to be overegotistical could be controlled by practicing poverty of spirit. It is noteworthy that Jesus did not suggest that anyone should be without spirit. Such would destroy individuality. He held that too much egotism is a personality disorder which needs to be checked by practicing poverty of spirit. Egotism breeds unhappiness, and Jesus wanted men to avoid it.

A classic illustration of egotism causing maladjustment is related in one of the parables. Jesus told a parable about some who trusted in themselves.

Two men went up into the temple to pray; the one a Pharisee, and the other a publican. The Pharisee stood and prayed thus with himself, God, I thank thee, that I am not as the rest of men, extortioners, unjust, adulterers, or even as this publican. I fast twice in the week; I give tithes of all that I get. But the publican, standing afar off, would not lift up so much as his eyes unto heaven, but smote his breast, saying, God, be thou merciful to me a sinner. I say unto you, This man went down to his house justified rather than the other: for everyone that exalteth himself shall be humbled; but he that humbleth himself shall be exalted" (Luke 18:10–14, ASV).

The maladjustment caused by this type of egotism is apparent. The imagined points of superiority were, in fact, elements of inferiority. One who does not actually feel inferior finds no necessity to defend or praise his virtues. The fact that a person feels the necessity of emphasizing his superiority means he really feels inferior. In cases such as this, egotism becomes a compensation for inferiority. It is, nonetheless, an area of maladjustment. It reveals a fundamental unhappiness with self. The fact that big men never feel big while small men never feel small continues to have psychological validity.

Jesus knew that unabated egotism could cause resentment, embarrassment, and unhappiness to men. He noted an egotistical practice taking place at feasts. And through the use of a pointed parable, Jesus showed how their egotism could get them into trouble.

Luke records the parable in these words:

And he spake a parable unto those that were bidden, when he marked how they chose out the chief seats; saying unto them, When thou art bidden of any man to a marriage feast, sit not down in the chief seat; lest haply a more honorable man than thou be bidden of him, and he that bade thee and him shall come and say to thee, Give this man place; and then thou shalt begin with shame to take the lowest place. But when thou art bidden, go and sit down in the lowest place; that when he that hath bidden thee cometh, he may say to thee, Friend, go up higher: then shalt thou have glory in the presence of all that sit at meat with thee. For every one that exalteth himself shall be humbled; and he that humbleth himself shall be exalted (Luke 14:7–11, ASV).

The practice of poverty of spirit not only helps avoid embarrassment but it also enables one to receive honors from others. It is basically true that men are prone to honor the humble and despise the self-seeking egotist.

It was obvious to Jesus that egotism is a form of selfishness which stresses the big I and the little you. He recognized that a person would and should have some self-interest. But he also taught that a person needs interest in many others if he is going to be happy with himself.

The seeds of nervous disorders grow to a full flower in an environment of egotism. When a supposedly mature person continues to practice the selfishness of some form of egotism, an expression of personality maladjustment is to be expected. Most people expect children to be selfish. The child thinks and acts solely in terms of my and mine. But too often he carries childishness over into his adult life with undiminished fury, proving again that biological maturity offers no assurance of psychological maturity.

Egotism expresses itself in many ways, but some aspect of childish selfishness is at the root of every form of it. It may stem from a desire to show off or to show up someone or to have one's own selfish way. No matter what form of expression it takes, egotism is basically a selfish response. It reveals the continuation of a childish method of adjustment. Unhappiness results.

One such expression of egotism was found in the following case history.

Tim had been obsessed with the idea of completing a prescribed course of study in a given period. Since he had a family, it was necessary for him to work. His plans included graduate work so it was necessary to keep up his grades. He tried to work full time and go to school full time at the same time. He thought his grades had to be perfect. When he fell from an A+ to an A in a subject, he regarded it almost equivalent to failure. As time passed, Tim drove himself even more. Naturally, his body rebelled, and a nervous condition developed. This condition was merely the symptom of his real problem.

Tim's basic element of maladjustment was childish egotism, though he did not recognize it. Others were completing the course in the prescribed time, so why shouldn't he? After all, if he could do it and work at the same time, would not it prove his ability for graduate work? So, Tim reasoned with himself and tried to explain away his egotism. Doubtless involved in the over-all problem were subconscious elements of his desire to show off.

Before the nervous condition came out into the open, Tim sought to fool himself with the notion that he had super-human endurance. Through bitter experience he learned differently. Too much unconscious egotism had been the driving force which caused a personality maladjustment. A little poverty of spirit along the way would have afforded a better adjustment to reality and would have kept the nervous condition from developing.

Ego weapons constitute another area of egotism causing maladjustment and discontent. An ego weapon may find any one of a number of outlets, but essentially it is a device to lord it over another. A few years ago an interim pastor found himself in the middle of a church squabble over the calling of a permanent pastor. The interim pastor made the mistake of choosing sides. For several weeks he preached on the Scriptures he thought would bring the other group into line. Of course, that group was not won over, but strangely enough his own group was the one helped. The hip pocket rulebook approach to religion is frequently little more than an ego weapon.

The automobile age has made childish egotism especially apparent. It is really remarkable how an otherwise mature adult can reveal hidden, infantile characteristics when he gets behind a steering wheel.

Take the case of Samuels. He is at least a fair driver, though he regards himself an excellent driver. Samuels is impatient. He drives furiously from one traffic light to the next. He constantly weaves from traffic lane to traffic lane. He runs up to the traffic light intersection and impatiently fidgets while waiting for the light to turn green. At precisely the moment it turns green, Samuels blasts his horn at the car ahead. He lurches forward and careens around the car ahead, barely missing the right rear fender. By the time he recovers from this fit of egotistical temper, the red traffic light just ahead catches him. But he steels himself again so he may continue to practice this homicidal ritual.

In due course he reaches the city. As Samuels is parking, he notices that the automobile which he almost rendered fenderless has just passed by. Although the automobile he almost destroyed was only a minute or so behind him, Samuels uses the alibi that he was in a hurry due to the press of business. He arrived in the city a nervous wreck. The other man, using more unselfish principles of driving, arrived about the same time. Samuels' alibi was an effort to hide the fact that he was expressing a selfish, childish egotism.

Two things are clear from this incident. Samuels' egotism did not give him any real advantage over the other driver. However, it did shake him up so that he was less effective on the job. He certainly was in no immediate frame of mind to be a constructive influence on people. It can be fairly said that a little poverty of spirit would have helped Samuels stand himself a little better.

Egotism sometimes expresses itself in perfectionism. This is one of the least sensible of all delusions. That any mortal with his vast areas of ignorance should suggest that he is the ideal of perfection is sheer nonsense. Yet, the would-be perfectionist regards his every action to be exactly proper and correct. Moreover, he demands that others meet his self-established standards of perfection. There are few people who please others in every detail. One attempting to do so is doomed to failure. It is hardly possible for a person to please even himself in full. But the perfectionist arbitrarily demands that his standards of perfection be met by others. This is a maladjustment arising from personal inferiority which is hidden in false egotistical superiority.

A typical case is noted in the man here called Steppen. He was a perfectionist de luxe. Steppen expected others to conform to his standards. Even the slightest deviation, he regarded as absolute sin. It had never occurred to him that no two people respond exactly alike in any situation. So, when people failed to meet his standards—and everyone did—Steppen scolded them furiously. His conduct was not calculated to do anything except to make him unhappy. Poverty of spirit is certainly his solution.

An egotist is especially open to imagined or real defeat as he is faced with the various problems of living. He deceives himself with the idea that he is self-sufficient. But his uncontrolled egotism shows that he actually is insufficient. Storms and stresses of life come to everyone. When they come to the egotist, he is defeated. He has trusted wholly in himself to solve every problem but finds he cannot do it. He has no one to whom he can turn because he recognizes no one as superior. So, his egotism has become a form of practical atheism by which self takes God's place. Self-centeredness has thereby become self-defeat. It has separated the egotist from his fellows and from God. Egotism has turned him from them.

Egotism in any of its forms and expressions causes some maladjustment and unhappiness. To some extent, depending on the degree involved, an egotist is unhappy with himself. He has separated himself from others and by putting himself out of touch with his fellow man, he is robbed of the opportunity to help others. His best single source of happiness and contentment is thereby lost.

It is evident that the one who is poor in spirit possesses something the egotist does not. He possesses personal stability, which is completely foreign to the egotist. Poverty of spirit is one of the building stones with which a blessed, happy, stable, secure life is built. These are absolutely essential to personality growth. It was no matter of mere empty moralizing when Jesus said, "Blessed are the poor in spirit: for theirs is the kingdom of heaven." They really have the kingdom already.

The poor in spirit are blessed, stable, adjusted. They now have the resources of heaven. It is significant that the very language itself shows the reward of the kingdom is already present. God cannot aid a person who realizes no need of help. The egotist realizes no need of help. He gets none. The poor in spirit recognizes his need of help; therefore, God can help him. The resources of the kingdom of heaven are not available to one who feels no need of them, but only to those who feel their need.

Many people regard the kingdom of heaven as a kind of external reward given those who merit it. Such a conception is clearly foreign to the idea here. As used here, it is generally regarded as the reign of God in the individual heart and life. Practical atheism, as fostered by egotism, precludes the reign of God in the heart and life. Poverty of spirit permits it. The recognized presence of God aids security.

Personality Cleansing

Psychologists have coined the term "catharsis" to describe personality cleansing. Actually, the word is a derivative from a Greek word meaning to purge or to cleanse.

It is presently held by psychologists that catharsis is necessary to a healthy, integrated personality. One of the basic practices used by psychiatrists today is the matter of personality or soul cleansing. Jesus advocated this same principle almost two thousand years ago. Often, emotional release is necessary. Jesus pointed out the basic blessedness of mourning and its comforting effect as tensions are released.

A fundamental premise in the psychology of human personality is that maladjustments arise because people do not understand, or will not face, their problems. Something happens that leads to unsolved conflict. This conflict is buried into the subconscious. A symbol of the conflict attaches itself to whatever a person is doing at that particular time. Hence, fears and tension become emotionally attached to the symbol of the maladjustment, and the real problem is hidden from consciousness.

The object of catharsis (personality cleansing) is to attempt to re-create the experience into consciousness. As soon as the experience is brought into the open, it is stripped of its terror. A person can look objectively at an experience in his conscious mind. But as long as it is below consciousness, terror, uncertainty, and maladjustment may arise.

That Jesus recognized the use of mourning for tension release and personality cleansing is evident in the second Beatitude. No, Jesus was not speaking metaphorically when he said, "Blessed are they that mourn: for they shall be comforted." He was emphasizing a psychological principle of adjustment necessary to happy, healthy mental life.

As used in the second Beatitude, mourning is the expression of personality seeking to avoid burying one's conflicts into subconsciousness. In this context mourning tends to bring the real conflict into consciousness. And to this extent mourning is an aid to stable thinking.

It is obvious that this kind of mourning is not mere fault-finding or fussing. Such tactics attempt to project the blame for one's difficulties upon others. Fussing recognizes no personal lack within one's self; mourning does.

Mourning is apparently universal. Sometimes it is an expression of conscious conflict raging within one's personality. Other times it breaks from within, seemingly through unconscious forces.

There are those who are unhappy and fussy because they do not have something they want. Maybe it is a new car, a new dress, or some other thing they covet.

Such an expression of unhappiness is not mourning. It admits no lack within the person. It merely calls attention to a selfish desire. An undue desire to obtain things comes from a craving within the ego to assert its selfishness. The unfortunate thing about this so-called mourning is that it can never be satisfied. There is no comfort for the craving of things. When the thing craved is secured, craving does not cease. It merely transfers itself to some other thing wanted.

Sometimes mourning is related to grief over the loss of loved ones. Grief under these circumstances may well be an evidence of a personal loss. Now, to the extent to which all types of sorrow lead to conscious consideration, this kind of mourning tends to result in consolation.

The mourning primarily emphasized in this Beatitude expresses a feeling of a personal lack. Such an attitude is hidden in mourning. Mourning is, therefore, a symptom suggesting the need to cleanse one's self from within. It seeks to help one bring out into his conscious thinking the fact of unconscious conflict within himself.

Occasionally morning may seem to be little more than a means to let off steam. But even this may have values to personality adjustment. It must be admitted that letting off steam can be very distasteful to others. Yet, in the proper surroundings such action can be an aid to catharsis for releasing one's tensions. Of course, there are better responses than letting off steam, but even this is better than repression. Naturally, conscious recognition and solution of the problem would be the best possible adjustment.

Guilt feelings may also be purged through mourning. The abnormal guilt feeling punishes a person long after the feeling has served its purpose. The guilt feeling tends to become repressed.

Now, the purpose of a guilt feeling is to stimulate one to take corrective action so that some thought or action may not linger unresolved in the subconscious and become a personality problem. But when the guilt feeling is repressed, it does not become a corrective step. Guilt may become as much of a problem to personality integration as the wrong that caused the guilt feeling. A guilt complex then develops, and corrective action is difficult, if not impossible.

The Beatitude asserts that blessed (adjusted, stable) are they who are mourning for they only shall be comforted. The imagery reflected in the mourning is that of wailing, as done at an Oriental funeral, and sustained or continuous mourning. The personal dissatisfaction involved in this kind of mourning generates its own capacity to receive the comfort that will surely come. There can be no comfort without mourning. Hidden within the mourning is the kind of comfort which will bring satisfaction.

Though the comfort is future, it is future only to the mourning; therefore, it may, and frequently does, immediately follow such mourning. It is interesting to note that Jesus said that the comfort would come from an outside agent. The word which has been translated "they shall be comforted" comes from the same root from which we get our English word "paraclete," or "comforter." It signifies that one has been called alongside of another in order to be of help. This is also from the same root of a word that Jesus used in speaking of the coming of the Holy Spirit as a comforter.

There is latent in the mourning a call for help and relief. The personal lack is so dissatisfying that it seeks help. With such an attitude of person, the outside agent, the comforter, can give the needed and desired relief.

Self-control

Stable personality has strength in gentleness. The person who has won the battle with himself is truly the strong person. Only those who confuse gentleness with weakness fail to realize that it takes more strength to be calm than to fly off the handle. It is a continuing psychological fact that self-control means mastery over self and situation. The wise one in the book of Proverbs put it like this: "He that is slow to anger is better than the mighty; And he that ruleth his spirit, than he that taketh a city" (Prov. 16:32, ASV).

Jesus said, "Blessed [adjusted, stable] are the meek: for they shall inherit the earth." But who are the meek? It is hardly probable that the current idea of meekness does any justice to this concept. No one can be stable when plagued with a sense of defeat. The notion now prevailing is that the meek are a withdrawing, cringing type like the Mr. Milquetoast of the cartoon. Involved here is an attitude of defeat. It is grossly wrong to think of meekness as a type of abject defeat. One suffering from such a complex certainly lacks self-control, which is far from the idea implied in this Beatitude.

The word "meek" which is used signifies one who is gentle, easy, or mild. The word was used in classical Greek to apply to a horse that had become gentle. The horse had yet all his fire and destructiveness, but it had been brought under control. Interestingly enough, the English word "gentleman" is meant to convey the idea of a gentle man. Self-control makes for gentleness. This is the idea of meekness. Here is a man with all the normal drives and instincts, but they have been harnessed and brought under control. A lack of self-control shows that a man has lost his biggest battle—the battle of self.

Stable or adjusted is the man who has brought the destructiveness of his drives or instincts under control. He has come to grips with the dynamic problems of sex, projection, etc., and controls them through sublimation or proper expression. He refuses to let the great physical instincts destroy his psychological development.

The control of self includes a harnessing of one's emotions. Uncontrolled emotions are not only distasteful to others but they are also dangerous to the well-being and inner harmony of the person involved.

Self-preservation is an instinct which is very valuable, but when it prompts revenge or bitterness, it is not harnessed. Likewise, each of the instincts is dangerous if expressed improperly. Such improper expression brings a definite personality weakness. Viewed in this light, meekness is the adjustment of one's self to one's self and becomes an aid to a stable, integrated personality.

To emphasize the importance of self-control, Jesus stressed the necessity of basic meekness. It is so important to self-control that those who are meek inherit the earth. Since the matter under discussion is personality adjustment, this expression is best understood to consider the function of the earth as man's environment.

It is from the environment that many stimulations come to

test a person's control of himself. In a real sense, adjustment to environment is an earth-conquering principle. Seen in this context, it is evident that meekness helps a person to possess the very things for which the earth was created.

A meek person has control of himself. The earth does not have control of him. The one who fails to effect self-control through meekness does not take charge of his environment; instead, his environment takes control of him. Surely, meekness is essential to personal adjustment.

Personal Desires

Every person has needs and desires. As the physical nature of man craves certain things, so the psychological nature of man has needs and desires also. The desires that lend stability to personality health are in the area of morals. It is interesting to note that such natural figures as hunger and thirst were used. "Blessed [stable, adjusted] are they that hunger and thirst after righteousness: for they shall be filled." Here is the person who craves the moral good. Here is a hunger whose satisfaction is certain. There is earnestness reflected. The present tense of the participles hungering and thirsting in the Greek shows that the craving is not occasional, but habitual and constant. Such an earnestness is certain to receive its reward. *The Expositor's Greek Testament* gives emphasis to this idea in the statement: "The hunger whose satisfaction is sure is that which contains its own satisfaction. It is the hunger for moral good. The passion for righteousness is righteousness in the deepest sense of the word." [1]

Those whose personal desires center around a quest for righteousness are the ones who are filled. The word means that they shall be made fat. It pictures satisfaction and contentment.

Probably more split personalities arise from a moral break-down within the personality than from any other cause. Seldom is the cause of the breakdown obvious to others. It seldom finds an outward expression, but an inward break-down of the person is very frequently more destructive than some outward expression. When it does find outward expression, it gives rise to some of the most hateful offenses against mankind. This Beatitude suggests a positive approach to mental hygiene. One with a craving for righteousness will have no place for the destructive elements of unrighteousness which would destroy his personality and life.

Mercy

Concern for others is essential to personal stability. There is an emphasis in one approach to so-called applied psychology which seeks to influence others from selfish intent. This emphasis is current today. We hear someone say, "I'll use psychology on him." Actually, such thinking is not psychology; it is sheer deception and hypocrisy.

To have real concern for the interests of others, selfishness must be put aside. Concern for others must be an end within itself, not a means to an end. False concern is quickly unmasked. The hypocrite loses whatever point of contact he had.

Concern for others—the practical result of mercy—expresses itself in many ways. Often it displays itself in concern for the physical needs of others—food, clothing, housing. But one of the most important ways to show mercy is by concern for the personal problems of others. A genuine concern to help another find the answer to his personal problems is a merciful attitude. An attempt is made to lead the person to help himself, not because of any benefit it may bring; yet, great benefit comes to one who practices this kind of mercy, for it makes him a stronger and more secure person.

Twentieth-century psychology? Yes, but it was first-century psychology, too. In the Beatitudes Jesus spoke about the psychological necessity of mercy.

The fifth Beatitude might well be paraphrased: Stable or adjusted are the merciful; for they [*only*] shall receive mercy. The teaching here is not a negative concept. It is no mere attitude of sympathy. It contains all the active elements of empathy, meaning to suffer with. Though lacking in pharisaic righteousness, the word "mercy" among the Jews generally embraced two things; namely, almsgiving and the pardon of injuries. These are two positive attitudes.

The Latin emphasizes the pain of heart. In each of these concepts there is a feeling in or suffering with the person affected. This is empathy. It is the placing of one's self into the other fellow's place and experiencing, to some extent, the experience as his own. It is a genuine concern for others with a determination to be of whatever assistance one can to another.

How is empathy, mercy, or compassion a basis for personal adjustment? The Beatitude explains that mercy is its own vehicle for the reception of mercy. Robertson, quoting Bruce, says, "A self acting law of the moral world." [2] It is the exercise or practice of this quality of mercy that tends to elicit mercy from others. One cannot have a friend who cannot be a friend. Likewise, one who is not merciful does not have the basis to receive mercy.

Mercy is a psychological necessity to the reception of mercy. This is well illustrated, historically, in the Pharisees. They failed to see that mercy was more important than strict legalism. They showed no real attitude of empathy toward others. This very lack of mercy made it impossible for them to appreciate and receive mercy. Jesus clearly revealed that only the merciful shall receive compassion. Mercy is an absolute necessity for mental health. Experience shows that everyone misses the mark. It is extremely difficult for one to adjust to the penalty of strict justice. Mercy aids in the process of adjustment.

Inner Integrity

Every person expresses a diversity of selves. He reveals himself as one person to his family, another to his friends, and still another to those with whom he is not acquainted. In some cases he may be trying to be deceptive. Other times it may be due largely to the interpretations of others. It may be that he has not intentionally caused the confusion. But, some people have deluded themselves with the notion that they can appear to be this or that, when in reality they are utterly different.

In the sixth Beatitude Jesus is teaching the necessity for inward (personal) purity and integrity as opposed to appearances. "Blessed [stable, adjusted] are the pure in heart: for they shall see God." The pure are those who are cleansed or purged of impurity. The area of the purity is that of the heart.

This word "heart" definitely is one which has greater meaning in biblical usage than elsewhere. Among the Jews it referred to the seat of personality. The Hebrew word "heart" includes the areas of the intellectual (rational), the emotional (aesthetic), and volitional (will) aspects of human personality. This concept was carried over into the New Testament. Therefore, "heart" in the Bible refers to the real personal nature of one's being.

The contrast is evident. This purity does not refer to external acts, but to the very thoughts, feelings, volitions, desires, motives. It is sincerity or singleness of heart as over against hypocrisy. As Lenski says, "It is the honesty which has no hidden motive, no selfish interest, and is true and open in all things." [3]

Impure thoughts, purposes, feelings cause personality decay. They enslave the personality. Only pure thoughts, purposes, and actions will render personality whole. These are crowded out by practice of impure ones. On the other hand, the way to eliminate an impurity in thought, feeling, or will is to crowd it out with the purer, stronger thought, feeling, or will.

Hypocrisy in one's relations is a destructive force. You cannot be adjusted or stable when you try to be other than yourself. You must be honest in all relations, but especially in all relations with yourself. This is the first principle of mental hygiene.

There is a close connection between clear vision and purity of heart. Personal purity is necessary for spiritual, personal perception. The expression "they shall see God" undoubtedly means that through purity of heart—inner integrity—one is made able for seeing, knowing, sensing the presence of God.

Such an enlarging awareness of God signifies a developing sense of personal fellowship. Most serious psychologists today recognize the necessity of a deep and abiding religious relationship as necessary to personal adjustment. Long ago Jesus emphasized the essential element of such a psychological imperative; namely, purity of heart.

Peacemaking

Personal stability is aided by peacemaking. This Beatitude "Blessed [adjusted, stable] are the peacemakers: for they shall be called sons of God" defines the status. No one can be stable whose personality is at war with itself, with fellow man, or with God.

This concept of peacemaking is no mere negative attitude. It is not to be regarded as a mere cessation of open hostility. One can be at war with self, others, and God and never do one overt thing to reveal it. Peacemaking is a positive, personal attitude of peace coupled with definite objective acts to promote peace.

The promotion and maintenance of peace has therapeutic value. Psychiatrists and psychologists advise those suffering certain neuroses and psychoses to find some cause they can serve. Jesus recognized that peacemaking not only lent stability to society but it also helped stabilize the participant. Clarke likely had this in mind when he said: "A peacemaker is a man who, being endowed with a generous public spirit, labors for the public good; and feels his own interests promoted in promoting that of others." [4]

A further stabilizing element in peacemaking is the recognition it affords. Peacemakers "shall be called sons of God." To be recognized as one of the sons of God gives a sense of belonging. It is an assurance of the security which comes from a feeling of belonging to a family. Such psychological security is essential to happiness, stability, and contentment.

Persecution

One seeks social acceptance. His social instinct—urge, drive, dynamic—craves acceptance by others. It finds satisfaction in acceptance and strives to achieve it.

Probably the most harassing element in persecution is that it amounts to the persecutor's personal rejection of the one who is being persecuted. It may not be so much the physical pain as it is the inevitable psychological pain that causes maladjustment or a feeling of rejection.

Jesus revealed that persecution can make a definite contribution to security if the persecution comes as an attack upon righteousness. There the primary attack is upon righteousness. The secondary attack is upon the person. But we have seen that righteousness is its own reward; therefore, the person affected by the persecution has the stabilizing element latent within the very persecution.

It is interesting to note the extent to which Jesus said the persecution may go. It may include insult, harassment, falsehood. It may involve every conceivable slander. Yet, if persecution comes on account of righteousness, it is a cause to rejoice and exult. Such a paradox would be most astonishing if it were not a fact that such unwarranted persecution can bring personal adjustment or blessedness.

When one is rejected through persecution on account of righteousness, he has real cause to rejoice. He is accepted by a greater one than his fellows. As an evidence of this acceptance, he is now in possession of the qualities of the kingdom of heaven. He now experiences the reign of God in the heart and life. He now has the forces of God's help which add to his blessedness, stability, happiness, adjustment, security.

Creative Self-expression

Two factors are necessary in the development of a strong personality. These are capacity and opportunity. A lack of either of these essentials will thwart development. Both are fundamental in self-realization and self-expression.

Self-expression can be either good or bad, either creative or destructive. Where it is the product of a motive to be of service to others, it is a healthy thing. Where self-expression springs from a desire to dominate others, it is an unhealthy, evil thing. That is true, regardless of how noble the activity itself may happen to be. Rollo May [5] has demonstrated this in his "ego weapon" concept. Does one excel in sports? Is this ability used merely for personal glory? If so, it is an ego weapon. Some men use their ability in business as an ego weapon rather than an opportunity to be of service to others. Some use their religion as a club rather than as a medium through which to be of service to others.

Jesus, speaking primarily to his students, laid the foundation for self-attainment and self-expression. There is not the slightest suggestion of a self-expression that would dominate. On the contrary, the element of service to others permeates the teaching. It is to be a service whose limits, if any, are coextensive with the earth and the world.

One may use the ability and the opportunity he has to be a positive, creative force. This is applicable, to a greater or lesser extent, with every individual. Most people have some ability and many opportunities for creative self-expression.

A child projects himself mainly with a self-centered motive. But he can also use this capacity for projecting himself in a creative manner. Where left to itself, capacity may be destructive; but if the drive is organized around a person other than one's self, it can become creative.

Examples of abnormalities arising from a self-expression that seeks to dominate are abundant. An end product of this is a type of self-delusion sometimes called paranoia. It finds expression in delusions of grandeur. A man thinks that he is a world figure. Therefore, he must impress the world with his importance by abnormal means. It is the sort of thing that gives rise to world conquerors. This delusion first begins as the unsolved personal problem. Then destructive self-expression is arbitrarily used to achieve domination over others.

An important symbol in the development of creative self-expression is represented under the figure of salt. The primary value of salt is its capacity to preserve. It is the nature of salt to maintain the *status quo*.

People, especially Christians, have a capacity like salt. They have the ability to increase their own stability by engaging in definite acts of service to others. It is abnormal not to use that capacity for service. Failure to use a capacity will result in its becoming insipid and useless. How can salt be salted? There is no salt of salt. What is not used for which it was intended loses its capacity for actual use. Whatever service one could be to mankind will be lost by nonuse and the individual becomes like saltless, insipid salt which is serviceable for nothing except to be "trodden under foot of men." It is said that insipid salt was used on the roads to minimize a hazardous road problem. Self-expression which does not express its capacity for service will, of course, cause problems to self and to others.

A second metaphor stresses another aspect of creative self-expression. This has to do with the nature and function of light. Again the element of service is evident. It is not the purpose of light to call attention to itself.

It is interesting to note that "Light of the world" was a title applied to the most eminent rabbis. Jesus applied this same concept to his disciples.

Light will shine if it has opportunity. Unless care be taken to hide the light, it will shine. Effort should not be taken to hide such light. This is stressed in three particulars. First, a city situated on a hill cannot be hid. That is an impossibility. Second, it is improbable that men would light their oil lamp and put it under a grain measure. Third, the sensible thing to do is to put a lamp upon a lamp stand in order that it may have opportunity to shine for all who are in the house. It is not light to call attention to self, but to shine to all who are in the house. Clarke has shown how the use of light under a measure was used by those who were possessed with evil designs. He reports: "From some ancient writers we learn, that only those who had bad designs hid a candle under a bushel; that in the dead of night, when all were asleep, they might rise up, and have light at hand to help them to effect their horrid purposes of murder." [6]

This light which ought to shine is described as creative in its very nature. Such light consists of noble and enduring service. The works are morally beautiful, commanding the admiring attention of others. This is the exact opposite of destructive self-expression. There is no attempt to dominate others in conduct that is noble and morally beautiful.

Here we have it, then—capacity and opportunity to express one's self, but to do so creatively. Though attention is necessarily called to the person who does noble works, such good works call attention mainly to one other than self. There is no attempt to glorify self. The good works are avenues of self-expression by which the Father who is in heaven may be glorified. This is creative self-expression.

3

Grow Up Socially

Think not that I came to destroy the law or the prophets: I came not to destroy, but to fulfil. For verily I say unto you, Till heaven and earth pass away, one jot or one tittle shall in no wise pass away from the law, till all things be accomplished. Whosoever therefore shall break one of these least commandments, and shall teach men so, shall be called least in the kingdom of heaven: but whosoever shall do and teach them, he shall be called great in the kingdom of heaven. For I say unto you, that except your righteousness shall exceed *the righteousness* of the scribes and Pharisees, ye shall in no wise enter into the kingdom of heaven.

Ye have heard that it was said to them of old time, Thou shalt not kill; and whosoever shall kill shall be in danger of the judgment: but I say unto you, that every one who is angry with his brother shall be in danger of the judgment; and whosoever shall say to his brother, Raca, shall be in danger of the council; and whosoever shall say, Thou fool, shall be in danger of the hell of fire. If therefore thou art offering thy gift at the altar, and there rememberest that thy brother hath aught against thee, leave there thy gift before the altar, and go thy way, first be reconciled to thy brother, and then come and offer thy gift. Agree with thine adversary quickly, while thou art with him in the way; lest haply the adversary deliver thee to the judge, and the judge deliver thee to the officer, and thou be cast into prison. Verily I say unto thee, Thou shalt by no means come out thence, till thou have paid the last farthing.

Ye have heard that it was said, Thou shalt not commit adultery: but I say unto you, that every one that looketh on a woman to lust after her hath committed adultery with her already in his heart. And if thy right eye causeth thee to stumble, pluck it out, and cast it from thee: for it is profitable for thee that one of thy members should perish, and not thy whole body be cast into hell. And if thy right hand causeth thee to stumble, cut it off, and cast it from thee: for it is profitable for thee that one of thy members should perish, and not thy whole body go into hell. It was said also, Whosoever shall put away his wife, let him give her a writing of divorcement: but I say unto you, that every one that putteth away his wife, saving for the cause of fornication, maketh her an adulteress: and whosoever shall marry her when she is put away committeth adultery.

Again, ye have heard that it was said to them of old time, Thou shalt not forswear thyself, but shalt perform unto the Lord thine oaths: but I say unto you, Swear not at all; neither by the heaven, for it is the throne of God; nor by the earth, for it is the footstool of his feet; nor by Jerusalem, for it is the city of the great King. Neither shalt thou swear by thy head, for thou canst not make one hair white or black. But let your speech be, Yea, yea; Nay, nay: and whatsoever is more than these is of the evil *one*.

Ye have heard that it was said, An eye for an eye, and a tooth for a tooth: but I say unto you, Resist not him that is evil: but whosoever smiteth thee on thy right cheek, turn to him the other also. And if any man would go to law with thee, and take away thy coat, let him have thy cloak also. And whosoever shall compel thee to go one mile, go with him two. Give to him that asketh thee, and from him that would borrow of thee turn not thou away.

Ye have heard that it was said, Thou shalt love thy neighbor, and hate thine enemy: but I say unto you, Love your enemies, and pray for them that persecute you; that ye may be sons of your Father who is in heaven: for he maketh his sun to rise on the evil and the good, and sendeth rain on the just and the unjust. For if ye love them that love you, what reward have ye? do not even the publicans the same? And if ye salute your brethren only, what do ye more *than others?* do not even the Gentiles the same? Ye therefore shall be perfect, as your heavenly Father is perfect (Matt. 5:17–48, ASV).

A HAPPY, secure person is one who is also socially adjusted. It is not so much the adjustment to places in the environment that counts as it is adjustment to other persons in the social situation. Of course, the neighborhood involved is sometimes the occasion that gives opportunity for the occasion of social maladjustment. However, this is merely symptomatic of a maladjustent more fundamental —one that arises because of a lack of adjustment to other people.

In the Sermon on the Mount, Jesus discussed several areas of social maladjustment. He also gave the remedy for such maladjustment. There is unfolded in Matthew 5:17–48 the progressive development of the aspects of social adjustment.

Childish Immaturity

Destruction is the product of immaturity. A child destroys without thinking. When the child matures properly, he puts away childish responses. Many people who have reached physical maturity still, at times, respond with infantile practices.

Physical growth is no guarantee of psychological development. There are those who have reached middle age whose responses are at the "strike-back" level of development. Both cold and hot wars are the all too tragic reminders of this condition. War is always an immature solution to a problem. This is a sad fact under which our enlightened civilization is chafing. Development is not aided by acts of destruction. It comes from a person's striving for maturity.

The people of Jesus' day had a very immature conception of the meaning of God's law. Their interpretation was strict, formal, legalistic. Jesus found it necessary to show them their need of development in their understanding of God's law. He told them he did not come to destroy the Law but to fulfil the Law. He came to give its fullest meaning through his interpretation.

Furthermore, many in Jesus' day thought that the Messiah would put aside the Law and set up a political reign by force. Some may have thought that, because of his talk of the kingdom of heaven, Jesus, to whom multitudes were rallying, had some revolutionary motive.

Destruction of the Law could not mean fulfilment. Not even the most insignificant part of the Law, viewed mechanically as the Pharisees and scribes viewed it by counting even the very letters, would pass away. Whoever should break one of the least of these commandments would be called least in the kingdom of heaven.

There is a stinging rebuke here to those who advocate that the end justifies the means. The kingdom was to come, but not through the efforts of an impatient reformer who would organize a political structure by a violent overthrow of the existing one. Such a procedure would show an immature analysis of the goal. Jesus did not destroy the Law; neither can any other and be happy and secure in his social relationships.

It is said that the strength of the British political organization in modern times lies in its ability to absorb change. It involves development without resorting to war as a necessary incident. Change is a condition essential to growth and maturity.

The principal weakness of the scribes and Pharisees was their self-righteousness. The elements of understanding, mercy, respect, and justice were disregarded. These elements are basically social. An attitude which does not give proper consideration to them is immature. One who would enter into the kingdom of heaven must have a righteousness that is developing, one which includes these social essentials. It must exceed the so-called righteousness of the scribes and Pharisees.

Conciliatory Nature

Murder is the result of anger or lack of interest in fellow man. This is true whether it is classed as premeditated or otherwise. Murder is an antisocial act as well as a crime. It has generally been regarded so from time immemorial. The ancient Jews, as well as others, had laws seeking to restrain the outward act of murder.

Murder is symptomatic of some social maladjustment which lies at the root of the physical act. Laws merely deal with the symptom, not the cause. Jesus knew that the things which lead up to murder actually are its cause. He sought to apply his remedy to the cause rather than the symptom.

With a psychological method that is as current as this morning's newspaper headlines, Jesus pointed out clearly those things in one's personal attitude which lead to murder. Then he gave a positive method which would eliminate the problem. Jesus first considered the problem negatively and then positively. He did more than merely name or define problems. He taught how to solve them.

Three things are fundamental in a bad attitude toward one's fellows: anger, contempt for another's ability, and contempt for another's character.

Anger is a personal product. No one can make another angry unless he is permitted to do so. Anger is an evidence of immaturity. Most anger results from some thwarting of infantile selfishness. Therefore, anger is a childish response to a situation. Every individual has some immaturity at this point, some more, some less. One should not permit himself to be defeated by anger. Then he will not be open to attack regarding his attitude toward fellow man.

Far from being a weakness, lack of anger is a strength of personality that few are able to attain. Jesus is one, however, who refused to let a situation constitute a basis of personal anger to the extent he could not have regard for others. Even when Jesus was cleansing the Temple, there is none of the get-even attitude in him.

Contempt for the ability of another is suggested in the untranslated word "raca." Probably this word could be fairly well translated by the current phrase "empty head." It is an attack upon one's ability. One does not have the proper attitude for another when he seeks to reduce him to an absurdity by the name-calling device. Though this practice is trivial in appearance, it is the source of much social maladjustment. It reveals social immaturity.

Contempt for one's character is expressed in the word that has been translated "thou fool." The term used is said to be a first-century Hebrew way of stating utter contempt for another's character. It is well interpreted by the expression "you scoundrel." Such an attitude of contempt reveals that a person is definitely alienated from another.

Adjustment to fellow man comes by way of compromise and conciliation. Compromise is the lifeblood of adjustment and progress. This is the positive approach. It removes the elements of a bad attitude leading to social maladjustment and murder. Conciliation is important to social adjustment. Though in the very act of offering a gift, one should leave his gift at the altar and get himself in good accord with someone who has something against him. This was calculated to astonish those religionists who thought that nothing should be allowed to disrupt acts of worship.

Positive reconciliation is basic not only to social adjustment but also to personal worship. No one can commit murder or other social wrongs who has a conciliatory nature. But a bad disposition toward another prevents adjustment to God and man.

The conciliatory mood is reflected not merely by a formal reconciliation but by one based on good personal feeling. This idea is demanded by the specific language construction in the original language. It may well be rendered "make it a habit of being kindly disposed and good minded." One who is "good minded" toward his adversary has refused to let an opportunity for maladjustment defeat him.

Too often one lets the delusion of the principle of the thing cause maladjustment. Much of the time this is an alibi mechanism under which personal pride is hidden. As Robertson says: "Compromise is better than prison where no principle is involved, but only personal interest. It is so easy to see principle where pride is involved." [1]

If one would avoid murder and other things which lead to this social maladjustment, he must rid himself of those things which cause bad attitudes. Such attitudes must be supplanted with actions that lead to good attitudes toward others. The difficulty is that people do not really believe that they are the authors of their own unhappiness. Very few really believe that to live in hatred, selfishness, or contempt closes the door to the kingdom as much as the act of murder, theft, or adultery. Likely, failure to take seriously the teachings of Jesus has been the roots for all social maladjustments.

Pure Nature

Purity in thought also has its social meaning. It is vital both for personal and social adjustments. One with impure thoughts and deeds for others always creates both personal and social maladjustment.

Within the range of adultery, lust, and divorce there is an evident lack of respect for others. There are three areas where the integrity of the personality of others is violated. Adultery is the definite act; lust is the seed for the adulterous act, while divorce constitutes the basis for placing the stigma of undesirability on another. Each of these makes social and personal security difficult.

The act of adultery was regarded by the Jews and other ancients as a violation of the peace and dignity of society. It was, therefore, punishable by law. But this looked toward the symptom rather than the cause, since only the actual act was held subject to the Law.

Adultery, however, has its beginning in personality that practices the purposeful, lustful look. The one who habitually or continually looks upon a woman to lust has already violated her. As far as he is concerned, a broken relationship already exists. She is already included within the purpose of his impure intent. To him, her personal integrity has already been violated. A healthy social adjustment is impossible in the face of such disrespect. Proper respect is impossible.

The source of the trouble is within the personality of the one who habitually lusts. The proper place to correct the wrong is at the source. If the heart were pure, lust would be impossible. Barry shows the psychological significance in the following quotation: "Once the suggestion has been really welcomed and worked into the substance of our lives, it is no longer under our control. It inevitably produces its effect. Our 'dominant desire' is our destiny." [2]

The solution to the problem of lust is suppression or sublimation—sublimation if possible; if not, suppression. Expression is not the solution. Such only accentuates lust. If one's right hand or right eye is the source of trouble, it would be better to lose the use of those parts than to destroy the whole person through improper expression.

It is astonishing that some psychologists have interpreted this as repression. There is much evidence that repression is a destroyer of personality, but not so with suppression and sublimation. These are constructive rather than destructive to a person's happiness and security.

Repression means the hiding away of something from consciousness. It is a mental attempt to duck the problem. Suppression and sublimation mean the very opposite. They bring the matter directly into consciousness and cope with it by a frontal attack.

Some psychologists have not been careful to distinguish between repression and suppression. Liebman [3] even went so far as to accuse Christianity of advocating repression. He thought that Jesus' teaching of lust and adultery's being equal was urging the practice of repression. Furthermore, Liebman felt that the over-all strategy employed by religion in the struggle against evil was nothing but repression, pure and simple. He believed that the practice was responsible for much grief, anxiety, and mental illness. What nonsense! This clearly misses the point of repression. There is no unconscious repression in that which is recognized and erased.

Weatherhead points out that there is a vast difference between repression and suppression. To the trained psychologist, "Do not repress" means to recognize and face what you are doing. To the untrained, it may mean "Do not suppress, do not exercise control." As Weatherhead says: "To say, 'Do not . . . exercise control . . . ,' is not only bad morally, but an invitation to license for which there is certainly no sanction in the science of psychology." [4]

The suppression suggested by Jesus meant the conscious, voluntary control of that which would create a problem. Improper expression of the sex instinct causes a greater problem than loss of its use. Jesus is generally regarded as the most adjusted of all men. He was tempted in all points like as others, yet without sin. Jesus, no doubt, suppressed and sublimated his sex drive.

Sublimation means the channeling of a drive away from its primitive aim into activities of a higher order. One drive can be sublimated with the doing of a stronger one. Jesus suggests in the "casting from" procedure that one drive can be channeled elsewhere by a stronger one. It is probable that the sublimation of Jesus took place in the area of the positive attitude of service he had toward his fellow man. And service to others is definitely a basis for social adjustment.

A disregard for the rights of others is seen in the teaching about divorce. Many Jews felt that divorce was permissible whenever they tired of their wives; hence, they regarded Moses' protective restriction as constituting the ground for license. Jesus said, however, that divorce had the effect of either condemning a woman to adultery or causing her to be regarded as an adulteress by society. Either of these amounts to social injustice.

It is to be remembered that divorce has the effect of embittering. Sometimes it causes one to have less regard for the other sex generally. Wholesale divorce cheapens human personality. All of this lessening of respect makes for poor social adjustment. The solution to this problem would be this. The woman should not be put away, except when she puts herself away by unfaithfulness. There would be no lack of respect in putting her away under those circumstances.

Truthful Nature

Deceit is also a symptom of social maladjustment. It has social meaning as well as being a basis of personal breakdown. Jesus' emphasis in Matthew 5:33–37 deals primarily with the social implications of dishonesty.

The people of Jesus' day practiced mental reservation in their dealings with others. Their method was to assure someone of the truth of their word while at the same time figuratively keeping their fingers crossed.

Jesus sought to show that one's word must be its own proof. If a man were disposed to deceit, any or all possible combined oaths could not give truth to his word.

This social emphasis does not apply primarily to the taking of oaths in court, but refers to a daily business practice. In order to attempt to prove his word about a statement or warranty in a business transaction, a man would resort to some oath. He might say, "I swear by my arm that this shop is a going concern." He would remember that his arm is not sacred, though his head is. Therefore, he is not bound to tell the truth. This was a deceptive way to get the best of the other fellow. The Jews had a whole series of such oaths of deception. Clarke offers a clear statement of the practice: "The morality of the Jews on this point was truly execrable: they maintained, that a man might swear with his lips, and annul it in the same moment in his heart. Rab. Akiba is quoted as an example of this kind of swearing." [5]

Jesus presented the negative side of the problem by telling them not to swear on this or that for any reason. They were to perform their oaths to the Lord. They were not to swear with reference to heaven, earth, head, or Jerusalem. These were things that were primarily God's domain. So, they did not become a basis for relationship between man and man. Someone has well said: "He, who swears by earth, either swears by God, or does not swear at all." Jesus wanted it clearly understood that all oaths were binding.

The positive approach to the problem is given. Instead of using an oath, one should say what he means and mean what he says. He should let his yes mean yes and his no mean no. What goes beyond this simple, nondeceptive way of dealing with others smacks of evil.

Truth is a very secure basis upon which to establish social relationships. The finest thing that can be said about a man by those who live in his community is that his word is as good as his bond. He is socially accepted both in business and other relationships. Truthfulness is an aid in doing away with social maladjustment. It helps one to grow up socially.

Loving Nature

A loving nature is the most complete basis of social adjustment known to man. Such a nature does not imply merely personal affection but something much more stable. It involves personal good will.

History has pointed out that men in their social development and adjustment have progressed, to some extent, through the following developments. First, there was the period of unlimited retaliation when the law of the jungle is said to have prevailed. Secondly, there was the period of limited retaliation when an eye for an eye meant not more than an eye for an eye. Thirdly, there was the period of limited love, emphasizing love for friends and neighbor. Finally, there was the period of unlimited love which emphasized love for enemies. The race is said to have passed through these ages. Yet, there are survivals of some of the more immature adjustments among men in every age.

Jesus laid the foundation for social adjustment on the basis of a loving nature with his negative and positive approaches to the problem.

The starting point for the development of loving nature is a nonretaliatory outlook. The law of eye for eye and tooth for tooth, even though itself a restraint, will not do. It is too negative. The positive approach to the problem is to turn the other cheek also. The evil referred to here has to do with personal differences of an insulting nature, rather than physical or moral evil. Jesus' counsel is for one not to let such differences get started in him. Here is another strength that few attain. Retaliation is to be elevated positively with love.

To make successful social adjustments, one must not only refrain from striking back but he also must display a lack of spite. One who is threatened with an unjust lawsuit usually has great difficulty in curbing his personal bitterness. This is the seed for revenge and the get-even policy. Here is the major point Jesus makes. One must not permit an injustice to render his personal attitude antisocial. It would be better to "give him thy cloak also." It is better to give up more than is asked than to let bitterness become a defeating problem to one's social adjustment. With clear psychological perception, John A. Broadus says:

It is matter of common observation in all ages, that a man who is threatened with an unjust lawsuit will show a peculiar animosity, and if he thinks himself unjustly treated in the sentence, a peculiar rancor and revengefulness, declaring that he will yet make his adversary suffer for it. Rather than feel and act thus, our Lord says it would be better even voluntarily to give far more than the aggressor is awarded. . . . How evil then must be this rancorous spirit.[6]

Social adjustment is further fostered by being noble. A generous spirit is a splendid help toward personal good will. If one is required to go one mile, go two. The practice pictured here was that of a Roman soldier requiring any person in the provinces other than a Roman to carry his military baggage for the space of one mile. To the Jew, this was a sort of slavery which was very insulting. The seed for maladjustment is evident. Jesus informed them that the way to whip this personal problem was to be generous; carry the pack an extra mile. Jesus' counsel helps to avoid a sullen spirit, harboring thoughts of revolt and spite. A man can change a burden into a blessing by doing more than is required of him. This is psychologically valid.

A benevolent attitude is likewise an aid to social adjustment. As a general rule, it is easier for an individual to have the proper regard for one he has done a kindness than for one he has not. When he has been of service to another, he is more likely to have an interest in that person than otherwise.

If one wishes a gift or a loan, do not turn away from him. The matter of the best interests of the borrower is not under consideration, only the matter of the adjustment of the would-be lender. Too often a person has contempt for one who wants to borrow. Not only does he fail to be of help but he also has a change in his former friendly relationship. This condition may be avoided by maintaining a benevolent attitude and practice.

A loving nature is much more than personal affection. In Jesus' statement "Love your enemies," there is to be found the meaning of this loving nature. This word "love" means personal good will. It is to be contrasted with the word "love" meaning personal affection. The word used here points out the need of one's having such personal good will toward all men. This is necessary if he would be happy and socially adjusted.

The true ideal is to hate no one. On the contrary, take positive action to avoid that pitfall. Pray for those who persecute you. Though this is an extremely difficult thing to do, its value to social adjustment is obvious. It is hard to pray for someone and be unhappy with them at the same time. Try it.

Personal good will should cause one to be fair and just in all his dealings with others. God "maketh his sun to rise on the evil and on the good, and sendeth rain on the just and on the unjust." God is just to men whether they deserve it or not. The late Dr. Conner, in his lectures to the Rural Education Conference at the Southwestern Baptist Theological Seminary, gave the emphasis exactly when he said, "God loves us in spite of the fact that he doesn't like everything about us."

But is not there some end to this matter of loving enemies? Not so far as one's adjustment to another is concerned. In the Greek, the present imperative of the verb means "love constantly." This means one is to go on loving and praying for those who offend him. One cannot be socially maladjusted who continues to pray for his enemies. This has a great psychological meaning for social adjustment, according to Clarke:

Jesus Christ designs to make men happy. Now he is necessarily miserable who hates another. Our Lord prohibits that only, which from its very nature, is opposed to man's happiness. This is therefore one of the most reasonable precepts in the universe.[7]

The teaching on social adjustment closes with a plea for maturity in social relationships. "Be ye [ye shall be] therefore perfect [mature], even as your Father which is in heaven is perfect" (KJV). The word "perfect" in this connection means "be growing up." It signifies striving for the ideal. Maturity is the ideal in social relationships. Destruction, retaliation, spite, hate are immature responses in any social situation. The immature respond to the social situation with destruction; the mature respond with love.

This is significant. Jesus' discussion of social adjustment began with a description of immaturity in social relationships and concluded with a statement of maturity. One must grow up socially if he is to be happy and secure.

4

Eliminate Spiritual Camouflage

Take heed that ye do not your righteousness before men, to be seen of them: else ye have no reward with your Father who is in heaven.

When therefore thou doest alms, sound not a trumpet before thee, as the hypocrites do in the synagogues and in the streets, that they may have glory of men. Verily I say unto you, They have received their reward. But when thou doest alms, let not thy left hand know what thy right hand doeth: that thine alms may be in secret: and thy Father who seeth in secret shall recompense thee.

And when ye pray, ye shall not be as the hypocrites: for they love to stand and pray in the synagogues and in the corners of the streets, that they may be seen of men. Verily I say unto you, They have received their reward. But thou, when thou prayest, enter into thine inner chamber, and having shut thy door, pray to thy Father who is in secret, and thy Father who seeth in secret shall recompense thee. And in praying use not vain repetitions, as the Gentiles do: for they think that they shall be heard for their much speaking. Be not therefore like unto them: for your Father knoweth what things ye have need of, before ye ask him. After this manner therefore pray ye: Our Father who art in heaven, Hallowed be thy name. Thy kingdom come. Thy will be done, as in heaven, so on earth. Give us this day our daily bread. And forgive us our debts, as we also have forgiven our debtors. And bring us not into temptation, but deliver us from the evil *one*. For if ye forgive men their trespasses, your heavenly Father will also forgive you. But if ye forgive not men their trespasses, neither will your Father forgive your trespasses.

Moreover when ye fast, be not, as the hypocrites, of a sad countenance: for they disfigure their faces, that they may be seen of men to fast. Verily I say unto you, They have received their reward. But thou, when thou fastest, anoint thy head, and wash thy face; that thou be not seen of men to fast, but of thy Father who is in secret: and thy Father, who seeth in secret, shall recompense thee (Matt. 6:1–18, ASV).

SPIRITUAL ADJUSTMENT implies more than a mere recognition of the existence of God. The fact that one believes in the existence of God does not mean that there is any personal relationship existing between him and God. A person believes in the existence of many things and people with whom he does not recognize a personal relationship.

Furthermore, spiritual adjustment means more than just open participation in outward acts that are said to be of a religious nature. Unless one recognizes the element of personal worship, an act of worship does not form the basis for a successful spiritual adjustment. It is spiritual camouflage.

Jesus considered three objective acts of worship to illustrate the necessity of personal relationship in the matter of spiritual adjustment. These three objective acts are the ones that the Jews regarded as the real heart of their religion; namely, giving, praying, and fasting.

The prime factor in the relationship of spiritual adjustment is that of the earnestness and sincerity of the worshiper. Sincerity is the keynote to personal spiritual adjustment. Though sincerity does not constitute the norm by which the validity of religion may always be measured, it does become the groundwork for individual spiritual worship. Certainly, this, beyond doubt, means that sincerity is needed for successful spiritual adjustment. This does not mean that some good will not be derived from engaging in religious acts. It means primarily that these acts will not develop a basis for personal worship without the element of personal sincerity involved. Other values will doubtless be received, but personal spiritual adjustment will not be gained. Such a relationship is reached only by the person seeking to relate himself in personal relationship with God. Psychologically, such is the norm of spiritual adjustment.

In order to be sincere a man must avoid religious parade. Putting on a show does not help his personal spiritual stability. If he performs his religious practices before men in order to be seen of them, he does not establish a relationship with God. He may get some rewards from men, but not from God. Since it has not been his purpose to worship, he has not done so. Even though the same act may be used by others for the purpose of worship, such spiritual camouflage does not help the insincere. It is significant that Jesus did not condemn the doing of religious acts before men. He counseled against them only if one's purpose was to be seen of men.

There are few things that aid the withdrawing person in the solution to his problems more than objective acts of worship and service. They have therapeutic value. So, these acts are not to be avoided unless one's supreme purpose for doing them is to be seen of men.

The Act of Giving

It has been said that the act of giving is found in every religion. Evidence shows that giving is a universal fact in all religion. The pagans far outdo Christians in this respect.

Probably the Jews were among the more careful people known to history in the regulation of acts of giving. The Hebrew people, not recognizing the principle of separation of church and state, collected tithes for the support of both, together with many other offerings. One who had failed to practice these acts consistently was said to have robbed God in tithes and offerings.

Regarding the specific practice of showing off that Jesus was criticizing, the authorities differ. Some say that the sounding of the trumpet in the streets was a public method of parading one's piety. It is said that he hired a brass band or trumpeter to lead the parade before him. This way he made known the fact that he was on his way to make a large gift. If this is so, he would be using the band for a fanfare to be seen of men. Other scholars deny that there is any evidence of this practice.

Again, some authorities hold that sounding the trumpet in the synagogue was accomplished in the following manner. It was said that the treasury consisted of a box having a funnel shaped, curved neck. In this coins were inserted. By dropping the coin in at a certain angle, it would rattle as it went round and round in the neck-like trumpet. A trumpeting noise was thereby made. Likewise, this practice is denied by other scholars. *The Expositor's Greek Testament* says that to "sound not a trumpet" is to be understood metaphorically.

Whatever may have been the background for Jesus' criticism, the inescapable conclusion is that he is condemning religious parade and spiritual camouflage in giving. Those who give to be seen of men are called hypocrites. They are like stage performers playing a part. The word "hypocrite" is described as a theatrical term. Greek theatrical performers in the course of a play might depict several characters. This was accomplished by the use of a different mask for each part portrayed. They were correctly called mask wearers.

Jesus characterized those who give to be seen of men as mask wearers. The *Cambridge Greek Testament* has a sound psychological interpretation when it defines the hypocrites as "those who play a part in life, whose actions are not the true reflection of their thoughts, whose religion is external and unreal. Such men begin by deceiving others, but end in self-deception." [1]

The insincere have received their reward and they have received it in full. Their purpose in giving was to be seen of men. They were seen by men. They got everything they sought. There is no reward from the Father who is in heaven because they did not seek a relationship in the first place. They sought none; they received none. This is the negative approach to the problem of spiritual adjustment in giving.

Jesus' positive approach to aid spiritual adjustment through giving is to avoid religious parade. Strive for this goal. When doing alms, if possible, do not permit the left hand to know what the right hand is doing. One who becomes concerned with the literal details of this statement misses the point. Jesus is not attributing to hands the capacity for knowledge. Such futile tangents hide the real psychological emphasis. Jesus is saying, through what has been called a bit of humor, that one should use extreme care to avoid insincerity in giving. A splendid psychological interpretation is found regarding this statement: "Let not even thy left hand, if possible even thyself, know, still less other men; give without self-consciousness or self-complacency, the root of ostentation." [2]

Sincerity in giving does not go unrewarded. By eliminating spiritual camouflage, it makes for personal happiness. The one who seeks spiritual adjustment in his giving does not go unrewarded. The better manuscripts referring to the reward do not contain the word "openly." The idea of being rewarded openly seems to violate the context because Jesus was not talking about public reward. He is speaking of an inward transaction throughout. The emphasis is upon spiritual adjustment through a sincere personal relationship in giving. To overlook this reward defeats the meaning of the passage.

When does the reward come, and what is its scope? *The Expositor's Greek Testament* has a significant statement about this: "The reward is present; not in the form of self-complacency, but in the form of spiritual health, like natural buoyancy, when all physical functions work well. A right-minded man is happy without reflecting why; it is the joy of living in summer sunshine and bracing mountain air." [3]

It is evident that sincerity of motive in giving will control the meaning of the entire act. Where one is seeking spiritual adjustment, the motive will also determine the size of the gift. The sincerity of the act of giving will determine the amount. Otherwise, the act of giving is not a personal aid in spiritual adjustment. Insincere giving is nothing more than spiritual camouflage.

The primary value in giving is psychological. Too many people, including some religious workers, have the notion that the primary purpose in giving is to promote or sustain religion. It is regarded as an obligation, more or less burdensome. But giving is a vehicle to spiritual relationship by which one can make his worship genuine. He can demonstrate clearly to himself at least that his motives are sincere and earnest. Viewed in this light, the act of giving becomes a privilege and a sound basis for one's spiritual adjustment.

The Act of Praying

Another area where religious maladjustment and spiritual camouflage abound is in the matter of prayer. All religions employ some forms or devices that are called prayer. The prayer book and the prayer wheel are well known to religious history.

The Jews of Jesus' day were subject to the same twofold criticism that might be leveled at much which is called prayer in this day.

Their prayer was faulty in purpose because it was insincere. In uttering words they were again playing a part—wearing a mask. Their purpose was not to establish a mutual relationship between themselves and God, rather, it was to establish their relationship with men. They were seeking to appear to be praying.

That they were primarily seeking the approval of men is shown by the places that they chose to do their praying—the intersections of the street and the synagogues. It is said that when it neared the hour of prayer, a Pharisee would hasten to the intersection of streets. It is evident that on the corner of the street they could be delightfully conspicuous from four directions. In the synagogues, as they stood, they could be seen by all present. Spiritual camouflage!

It is obvious that public prayer is not disapproved. It is only when men parade their piety before others to be seen of them that a practice claimed to be public prayer is bad.

A man is what he does when he is alone. Jesus, assuming men would pray, strove to emphasize the importance of personal, secret prayer as a move toward spiritual adjustment. When one prays, he should seek to shut out everyone else, even one's self as much as possible.

The decisive things in real prayer are the inner motives and the attitudes of the person praying. Yet, spiritual camouflage covers up the inner man in favor of the outward act. To let the outward act pass for one's intent and purpose results in imitation and mockery.

Sincere, purposeful, individual prayer is seen by the Father who sees in secret. Such prayer is primarily to the Father. He takes notice of it. The reward, which must surely come, is religious adjustment. This is acquired by the personal relationship established through sincere prayer.

A second fault of the pharisaical prayer was its faulty content. It consisted of vain, empty repetitions. In this respect it was like that of the heathen, whose idea is to use many words. By an abundance of words and empty repetitions, they can advise their gods of their needs and harass them into granting their petitions.

Something of this idea of empty repetition is found in the use of the pagan prayer wheel. This prayer wheel has slits cut out in its edge. In these little pieces of paper may be inserted containing prayers. Each time the wheel spins and one of these papers completes the circle, a prayer is said. By inserting several pieces of paper and by spinning the wheel fast, one can get a large amount of praying done without personal participation. The counting of beads as prayers keeps current the pagan idea of quantity rather than quality in prayer.

It is Clarke who sounds the psychological note on the use of vain repetitions in prayer when he says, "Prayer requires more of the heart than the tongue. The eloquence of prayer consists in the fervency of desire, and the simplicity of faith." [4]

It is not necessary to advise God about our needs, "for your Father knoweth what things ye have need of, before ye ask him." The question then arises, why pray? What is the purpose of prayer? The answer to this question reveals clearly a vital problem to spiritual adjustment through prayer.

The naïve and somewhat pagan idea is that prayer is a device to tell God what one wants. The next step is to insist that God provide one's wants in one's own way. This is the idea of prayer as a string-pulling device in which God is obliged to perform as a mechanical robot. This concept regards prayer as a mechanical changer in which a violation of the normal order of things is insisted upon. Any other interpretation of prayer is regarded as casting a reflection on God. The truth of the matter is that this naïve interpretation of prayer casts a reflection upon God. Such thinking would make it necessary for God to step in and modify things in his creation at the whim of the one who asks him to.

This practice is all too evident when one recalls that there are those who would pray for rain while others, at the same time, would pray for it not to rain. Under circumstances such as these, whom shall God answer? The absurdity of the situation is apparent. Better would it be for both parties to pray with the attitude that there is ground for personal spiritual adjustment whether it rains or not.

Fortunately, the natural laws providing for rain are organized on a more secure basis than what John Doe and Richard Roe think advisable for their personal interests at any given time.

But again, why pray? From a psychological viewpoint prayer conditions one for the inevitable. The main thing in prayer is not to get things but to get the person in fellowship with God. Prayer conditions one to God. It opens up a man's heart and permits God to come in.

Care must be exercised not to permit any occasion to be the excuse for a break in fellowship with God. Prayer permits adjustment to the problems of life. It establishes fellowship with God and assures the person praying that there is a basis for adjustment to any situation.

Prayer also has therapeutic value since it brings about

personality control. Something of this concept is held by
Stolz when he says: "Now prayer is a form of personality
control, an act whereby vital power is made available and
organized. As such, prayer reduces tension and furthers the
integration of personality." [5]

By way of contrast, Jesus shows what prayer is not and
then shows what true prayer is. In regard to what prayer is
not, Jesus gives in a brief statement his summary. Prayer is
not putting on a theatrical performance. It does not consist
in saying words. The length of the prayer has nothing to do
with it. Prayer does not consist of an attempt to instruct God
with wishes and needs. Prayer does not change God. It
changes man so that he may be in harmony with God.

Chamberlain [6] and others have held that positive prayer
consists primarily of certain attitudes of soul or personality.
True prayer eliminates the spiritual camouflage, faulty purpose, and faulty content. It relates the inner person positively through several psychological dispositions of mind,
heart, and action. These dispositions or attitudes are the very
substance of real prayer. Through them the "I—Thou" relationship is genuinely established.

Jesus outlined the elements of real prayer in less than sixty
words. With these few words he gave men a manner of
prayer about which countless words have been written. The
words of Jesus' model prayer are few, but the psychological
meaning is inexhaustible. An analysis will quickly reveal
some of its psychological content for spiritual adjustment.
The personal elements of true prayer include some of the
following ideas.

First, genuine prayer contains the element of personal
trust. How foreign this was to the pagan idea that the gods
must be placated or bought off. Jesus said, when you pray
have in your heart the concept, "Our Father, which art in

heaven." What meaning? Trust! Jesus meant for men to regard God not as a selfish, disinterested person who must be bought off but as a father. All the confidence and trust a little child has toward a father is implied.

But more! He intended for mankind to regard God as a Heavenly Father, unaffected by human selfishness, poor judgment, lack of knowledge, or other human, finite limitations. The starting point for any genuine relationship with God is trust and confidence in God. Spiritual camouflage cannot develop into an atmosphere of trust.

Second, an element of reverence is the soul of true prayer. Jesus said the prayer should contain this disposition of heart. Here are his words: "Hallowed be thy name." The word "hallowed" basically means "set apart, sanctified." Reverence is essential to a proper regard for God. It is also a psychological necessity for a vital personal relationship between man and God.

Third, note the element of submission. The element is found in the words "Thy kingdom come. Thy will be done, as in heaven, so on earth." It recognizes the will of God and one's subjection to it. Subordination to God is essential to stability and security.

Fourth, observe the element of dependence. "Give us this day our daily bread" reveals the attribute. The word for daily bread was one referring to the amount of food given to a slave. He was given only enough food for one day at a time. This practice minimized his opportunity for escape. In like manner, one's attitude in prayer should recognize dependence upon God for the needful food for just the one day at hand. It is a recognition of daily dependence upon God.

Fifth, there is the element of forgiveness. This attitude permits God's forgiveness, since the petitioner has already forgiven those who are indebted to him. The petition is "and forgive us our debts, as we forgive our debtors." It is psychologically true that to receive forgiveness, one must forgive.

Sixth, the element of humility is essential. Jesus describes this attribute both negatively and positively. Negatively it is stated, "Lead us not into temptation," positively stated, "Deliver us from evil." The petitioner recognizes the humble position he occupies in these transactions. It is God who can guide and lead; the petitioner merely follows.

Likely, the temptation mentioned here is that of moral trial. This must be distinguished from the eighth Beatitude. In that Beatitude the persecution or trial is from without. It is externally applied. In the petition of this prayer the evil is that of moral evil, which results from moral compromise and is from within. The psychology of the process of temptation has been clearly described.

The process of temptation is often as follows: First, a simple evil thought. Secondly, A strong imagination or impression made on the imagination, by the thing to which we are tempted. Thirdly, Delight in viewing it. Fourthly, Consent of the will to perform it. Thus lust is conceived, sin is finished, and death brought forth, [i.e., death to some aspect of human personality]. A man may be tempted without entering into the temptation: entering into it implies giving way, closing in with, and embracing temptation.[7]

To consider the psychology of prayer raises the danger of thinking that prayer is only subjective, since the main purpose is to condition man to the inevitable. Because of this fact, some have held that there is no objective reality in prayer, only subjective force. To these interpreters, prayer is a sort of escape mechanism. They regard the person himself as the center of reference.

But this interpretation implies a sort of dualism. One nature of the individual deludes the other nature of the same individual into thinking he has acquired some value from the act of prayer. Such is the logical product of a psychology of prayer that regards it only from the standpoint of its effect upon the one engaging in prayer.

There is another side to prayer that must not be overlooked if it is to be understood properly. This other matter is that prayer must be well grounded in the objective reality of the relationship of the "I and the Thou."

Many books on the psychology of religion point out the significance of the objective reality of God in prayer. Hardly a clearer treatment can be found than that written by Snowden a number of years ago. He firmly believes that prayer is grounded in the objective reality of the relation between the soul and God. Faith that one's prayers reach God and become a part of his plan causes him to answer them, not according to our desires only, but according to his wisdom.

The subjective value of prayer is a vital force; but if one believes this is all there is involved, he does not really pray. As Snowden says:

We cannot continue to believe and practice with the heart what we have rejected with the head. We can no more rise above ourselves in prayer that is only a subjective state, than we can lift ourselves to the stars by pulling on the hair of our heads. Such prayer is only a soliloquy. When its secret is discovered, it will cease to be rational and respectable. And so psychology no less than scripture affirms that he who comes to God must believe that he is, and that he is a rewarder of them that diligently seek him.[8]

It is in the reality of the relationship between God and the one who is praying that the ground for the result of sincere prayer—personal assurance—is found. Without such an assurance of its objective reality, prayer cannot be a vehicle to spiritual adjustment. With such an assurance, sincere, meaningful prayer may be such an aid to happiness and security. Happily, true prayer helps avoid spiritual camouflage.

The Act of Fasting

The practice of fasting has a very interesting history in its development among the Jews. It seems that at first, fasting was the natural expression for grief or great concern. It is said that Hannah, because of her barrenness "wept, and did not eat" (1 Sam. 1:7). David employed fasting to show others his grief at Abner's death. Again, David seems to have used fasting before the death of his child to give more sincerity to his prayer. There are references in the Old Testament where fasting was designed to be of national scope in case of war or pestilence. References of national fasting due to war are found in Judges 20:26, and 2 Chronicles 20:3.

It will be observed that with such practices fasting became recognized as a method of seeking divine favor and protection. From this concept there followed the association of fasting with the confession of sin—fasting becoming an outward evidence of penitence. Fasting was often of varying duration and varying content.

By the time of Jesus, the Jews had many regulations for the practice of fasting. They sought to enforce fasting in a mechanical way without regard to the spiritual condition of the one fasting.

Where fasting results from the force of outside pressure, it is rather to be expected that other distortions will arise. Such distortions as personal insincerity, however, tend to violate the personality.

The thing that Jesus condemned was not the practice of fasting, but the Jew's personal purpose in fasting; namely, to be seen of men. In the normal course of things Jesus knew that they would fast. There would be times when food would become secondary. He did not command them to fast.

Jesus told them that when they did fast to take definite steps not to appear to be fasting. They were told not to be like the hypocritical mask wearers. In pharisaic practice, fasting, like prayer, had been reduced to a system. They were to fast twice a week—on Thursday, the day of the ascent of Moses, and on Monday, the day of his descent from Mount Sinai.

The position of Jesus was that for a fast to have any spiritual value, it must be primarily between man and God. When Jesus had the temptation experience early in his ministry, he fasted forty days and nights. This fasting grew out of a situation which was so intense that food became secondary. He was not hungry. His fasting was the result of his spiritual adjustment to God's will rather than the cause of his adjustment.

Sincere fasting is encouraged. The one who fasts in secret will not be without his reward. This reward will be in the area of spiritual and personal adjustment.

Whether Christianity, as developed in its Western movement, has been wise in causing the virtual extinction of the practice of fasting is questionable. One thing, however, remains evident. Fasting, or any other outward act, must be sincere—possibly also spontaneous—if it is to be of aid in spiritual adjustment. One's mental hygiene demands that he avoid spiritual camouflage in this and every other religious thought and act.

5

Defeat Neurotic Anxiety

Lay not up for yourselves treasures upon the earth, where moth and rust consume, and where thieves break through and steal: but lay up for yourselves treasures in heaven, where neither moth nor rust doth consume, and where thieves do not break through nor steal: for where thy treasure is, there will thy heart be also. The lamp of the body is the eye: if therefore thine eye be single, thy whole body shall be full of light. But if thine eye be evil, thy whole body shall be full of darkness. If therefore the light that is in thee be darkness, how great is the darkness! No man can serve two masters: for either he will hate the one, and love the other; or else he will hold to one, and despise the other. Ye cannot serve God and mammon. Therefore I say unto you, Be not anxious for your life, what ye shall eat, or what ye shall drink; nor yet for your body, what ye shall put on. Is not the life more than the food, and the body than the raiment? Behold the birds of the heaven, that they sow not, neither do they reap, nor gather into barns; and your heavenly Father feedeth them. Are not ye of much more value than they? And which of you by being anxious can add one cubit unto the measure of his life? And why are ye anxious concerning raiment? Consider the lilies of the field, how they grow; they toil not, neither do they spin: yet I say unto you, that even Solomon in all his glory was not arrayed like one of these. But if God doth so clothe the grass of the field, which to-day is, and to-morrow is cast into the oven, *shall he* not much more *clothe* you, O ye of little faith? Be not therefore anxious, saying, What shall we eat? or, What shall we drink? or, Wherewithal shall we be clothed? For after all these things do the Gentiles seek; for your heavenly Father knoweth that ye have need of all these things. But seek ye first his kingdom, and his righteousness; and all these things shall be added unto you. Be not therefore anxious for the morrow: for the morrow will be anxious for itself. Sufficient unto the day is the evil thereof (Matt. 6:19–34, ASV).

THE STUDY of fear is both fascinating and profitable. Probably no other emotion has the ability to do as much good or as much harm as fear. Fear can be either constructive or destructive to human personality. A healthy fear is a protective response while abnormal fear is very unhealthy.

To some, the mention of fear in connection with the spiritual personal nature of man gives opportunity for the venting of a personal prejudice; namely, that religion is grounded in fear. The position taken is that religion has its origin and development in fear. This is assumed to be true with the prehistoric man and also with the present-day religionist.

Johnson's research reveals that fear is a nonessential element to religion itself. He thinks the notion that fear is the primary emotion has been utterly displaced. Johnson concludes that if fear was evident in primitive religion it was not because of its intrinsic qualities, but because of the insecurity and the danger which dominated primitive life. Even so, fear becomes modified by other emotions. Says Johnson, "In the emotional progression of religion, fear changes to awe, reverence, admiration, gratitude, and a sense of the sublime. And in the higher civilizations today fear and awe have been largely displaced by other religious emotions." [1]

It does not appear to have occurred to Jesus that fear constituted the basic reason for the worship of God. On the contrary, Jesus showed how the abnormal expression of fears—anxiety, worry, and phobias—rather than being of aid were definitely detrimental to human personality. He sought to show that faith, not fear, was primary in the establishment of healthy adjustment and relationship.

A healthy fear is obviously protective. This kind of fear permits the adjustment to environment and to things that arise outside of the self. Many examples of protective fear are evident. Remember those times the empty sign on the gasoline register caused you to dart into the first service station at hand? What about the times you have gotten up in the middle of the night to look in on the children "just to be sure"? Or what about those feelings of anxiety that develop when you are not sure that you have turned off the gas? Do you hurry back into the house to check it? You surely do!

Similarly, fear of fire, disease, tornado, or the like will dictate precaution. Fear of famine caused men to start saving. Fear of drouth gave rise to the development of irrigation. Fear of storms brought the development of substantial construction. Such fears are constructive so long as men do not permit them to become abnormal problems. When they do, a demoralizing phobia has been born.

It is not the healthy fear that Jesus is concerned with in this teaching. He is dealing with those abnormal fears which arise from daily living—fears that are related to what latest gadgets we have or have not.

The prevalence of such fears was well illustrated by a recent speaker who said that the old are afraid to die, and the young are afraid of life; the unlearned are afraid because they do not know, and the learned are afraid of what they do know; the poor are afraid because they have no money, and the rich are afraid because they have. In these, and like situations, it is not fear of the thing itself that causes the problem. Rather, it is because no solution is apparent.

It might be said, by way of parenthesis, that to the one

who fears fear, an escape from the symptom of fear will not solve the problem. Such escape will merely intensify the problem and permit it to spring up clothed in something else.

Fear of fear reminds one of Jesus' description of the unclean spirit. When this spirit has gone out of a man, he passes through waterless places seeking rest. He cannot find it, so he returns to the house and finds it empty, swept, and garnished. Then he takes with him seven other spirits, more evil than he to enter and dwell therein. So the last state of that man is worse than the first. Fear of fear is itself a similar multiproblem to happiness, stability, and security.

The greatest single cause of unhappiness and maladjustment is abnormal fear. Fear is at the base of every mental illness, whether such illness has an organic basis or not. Patients in institutions or under the private care of doctors or psychiatrists are often primarily sick with fear. They need help.

Jesus was concerned with those factors in human personality that are so often the cause of abnormal fears. He clearly defined the causes of abnormal fears which plague and destroy men. Generally, there are four basic forces which breed abnormal fears and neurotic anxiety in the hearts of men. These include a false sense of values, double-mindedness, the divided life, and fear of fear.

False Sense of Values

The by-products of materialism are evident in every generation. In philosophy, materialism continues to have its adherents. In the other arts and also the sciences, the effect is felt. It is so far-reaching that religion is not left untouched, and history knows of religious materialism.

Materialism is a subtle force that pervades every area of existence. It does not confine itself to the speculative but takes its toll in the areas of the practical as well. It is no wonder, therefore, that materialism should try to attach its spirit to the practical ramifications of human personality.

The product of materialism in the workaday world of men is seen in their false sense of values. Under this influence men acquire worldly aims and begin laying up treasures on earth. Material considerations become the basic treasure of life. Their purpose becomes fixed upon attitude and conduct. Things become an end or goal rather than a means to a more enduring end.

Since material treasures are corruptible and transitory, it is utter self-deception to regard them as enduring values or a secure basis upon which to fix one's dominant motive in life.

Abnormal fear may readily come to anyone who has such a false sense of values. The insecurity of the situation is apparent in the very nature of the treasures sought. They cannot last. Realizing that men were destroying their personality with such empty treasures, Jesus counseled:

Lay not up for yourselves treasures upon the earth, where moth and rust consume, and where thieves break through and steal: but lay up for yourselves treasures in heaven, where neither moth nor rust doth consume, and where thieves do not break through nor steal: for where thy treasure is, there will thy heart be also (Matt. 6:19-21, ASV).

One who regards the material as being of real value treasures it. He seeks it. What your treasure is will dominate your personality. Jesus said, "For where thy treasure is, there will thy heart be also." All of one's personal being—intellect, emotion, action—will be sacrificed on materialism's altar of self-deception.

Lenski sounds the psychological note which shows this basis for fear when he says: "Graphically Jesus brings out the self-deception. To treasure treasures that take wings and disappear, 'to make to vanish,' 'to take from sight,' is to deceive and cheat oneself. You think you have treasures and in reality you do not have them." [2]

Treasure of personality is vastly more desirable than material treasure. Personality is the only lasting value in existence. Therefore, one should start treasuring up heavenly treasures which are not subject to dissipation, destruction, or theft.

It is extremely doubtful that Jesus is talking about external rewards to be bestowed hereafter. Such an idea does not satisfy the demands of the context. The anxiety caused by the materialistic motive is a present reality. If it is to be corrected, it must be now. These heavenly treasures must therefore be in the area of the personal development, such as the loss of this demoralizing fear. To acquire a valid sense of values is a heavenly treasure in its own right.

Furthermore, the context of the entire passage is not satisfied with an interpretation of "laying up treasures" as having to do with acts of benevolence, service, or the like. Except insofar as these acts are sources of treasure to the personality within themselves, they are not involved here. The point to be made is that as these personality treasures develop they are abiding, incorruptible, and cannot be taken away. These are the heavenly treasures.

The technical objection to the phrase "in heaven" not meaning "heavenly" in the grammatical sense is well met by *The Expositor's Greek Testament* which says, "Grammatically, this is correct, yet practically, heavenly treasure is meant." [3]

Men diminish their abnormal fear which is conditioned on a false sense of values. They acquire a new sense of values which gives supreme importance to human personality. Instead of making the materialistic aim the dominant motive in life, one should make the development of human personality in his own being, and in others, the dominant motive in life. This is truly treasuring heavenly treasures.

Seldom has anyone so clearly seen the destructive effect of a false sense of values upon human personality as has Weatherhead. In a work [4] of a few years ago, he pointed out that men must get their sense of values right. A false sense of values is utterly contrary to the best interest of one's peace of mind and inward harmony.

Double-mindedness

A second prevalent cause of abnormal fear is in the matter of double-mindedness. The single eye was a current expression in Jesus' day, referring to soundness on the physical side or simplicity on the spiritual, personal side. This was an extended significance given to a concept among the ancient Jews that an evil eye denoted an envious, grasping man. In effect, the good eye meant a beautiful heart, while an evil eye meant a covetous heart.

If the eye is single, the whole body will be full of light. It will be filled with understanding. But if the eye is evil, the whole body, or the entire personality, will be filled with the darkness of self-deception.

Abnormal fears thrive in the person who is without understanding. They seem to diminish when they are recognized and understood, but where the eye be evil, the double-mindedness in personality will not permit clear understanding.

Covetousness is an expression of insecurity. It is basically the expression of abnormal fear, stemming from selfishness. Of course, selfishness is itself another expression of insecurity. Covetousness is thus seen in its true perspective as an abnormal fear response.

The single eye is not divided. If the eye is single, one's whole personality will be light. He will have understanding. So he will have this added protection against abnormal fear.

The Divided Life

There is a third form of self-deception which nourishes abnormal fear. This is displayed in the divided life. Jesus is recorded on this matter as having said, "No man can serve two masters." It is literally translated "No man can be a slave to two masters." This statement reflects the practice, current in Jesus' day, of personal ownership of human beings. It was legally impossible for a slave to be owned by two distinct masters, since it could create an impossible situation for the slave. He could hardly obey two masters at the same time.

Similarly, no man can bear allegiance to two opposing forces that seek his all. He cannot be a slave to both God and mammon. He cannot serve those forces of God which claim his attention and at the same time serve the forces of mammon. Any attempt to do so must inevitably give rise to a division in personality. As Lenski says, "The cunning, which would try to divide its devotion and its service between these two masters, cannot possibly succeed; it only deceives itself." [5]

The desire to serve others versus the desire to serve self frequently causes a conflict. The desire to serve others is of God, while the desire to serve self is of mammon. The divided personality naturally follows where an attempt is made to serve both. Barry expresses the psychological import as he says,

A conflict must inevitably arise. One may centre round the service of his fellows (the social instinct is at the root of it) and the other round his personal ambition (with the self-assertive instinct as its driving power). The two systems are incompatible. Hence arises the familiar story of the divided life.[6]

A divided personality is a perfect habitat for abnormal fears. The reason for attempting to serve antithetical forces is doubtless because of fear of one of them. The conflict of loyalties is at the least a symptom of abnormal fear.

Obviously, this divided thought and action develops the divided life. Such is the wages of an abnormal fear.

One thing appears evident in all three of these areas of abnormal fear. This is the matter of selfishness. It is apparent in a false sense of values, in double-mindedness, and in the divided personality. The selfish life always centers around the self, and the constant fear of being thwarted in some selfish expression seeks protection. This is the defensive mechanism of abnormal fear at work.

Fears that are not grounded in objective reality are none-theless real to those who possess abnormal fears. It is seldom of aid, and often quite disasterous, to advise one to forget his fears with the counsel to "buck up, it's all in your mind." What the person needs is someone to help him analyze and understand his fears, not to tell him to forget them. Forget-ting fears is impossible; such an attempt ends in repression. It is reasonable to say that understood fears do not often constitute personal problems as do those not understood.

Significantly, Jesus does not advise one to forget his fears and anxieties. He seeks to encourage their being brought out into the open for consideration from several points of view. In this way, one may find ground to assure himself that his fears are not founded upon real fact. It does not help much to be so assured by others; but where one can assure him-self that his pathological fears are groundless, he has gone a long way toward their solution. The fallacy of an abnormal fear must be self-determined before there can be a solution to the problem.

In an attempt to get a person to examine his fears honestly, Jesus used a number of analogies that show abnormal fears in their proper light. The practical problems which confront men, such as anxiety over food, drink, and clothing, are considered as occasions to abnormal fear. These are fundamental, though they may be subject to some modification among the different cultures.

It is a known fact that life consists of something more than the material which sustains it. Since God gave life, it is reasonable to suppose that God can be trusted to sustain it. If this be true, there is no valid, objective reason for worrying about food and clothing.

The logical position into which Jesus is leading precludes the notion that Jesus' statement is one of folly. He is not advising men to cease giving any consideration to food and clothing. He is teaching them not to be distracted or anxious about these matters. They are not to become a problem. Clarke displays clear psychological perception when he says, "Prudent care is never forbidden by our Lord, but only the anxious distracting solicitude, which, by dividing the mind, and drawing it in different ways, renders it utterly incapable of attending to any solemn or important concern." [7]

The philosophical syllogism is employed to show the needlessness of neurotic anxiety and distraction. In his analogy of the birds, Jesus leads into this syllogism: Major premise—God feeds birds; Minor premise—people are more important than birds; Conclusion—therefore, God can be trusted for sustenance. Anxiety and distraction are utterly needless.

Furthermore, anxiety is also useless. No amount of it will add one cubit to the span of life. It does not actually change anything in the outward situation, but, as Robertson says, "Anxiety will not help either kind of growth [height or length of life], but rather [it will] hinder by autointoxication if nothing more." [8]

To "consider the lilies" is another outward thought that Jesus would have the unduly anxious person use to analyze and understand his abnormal fears. Here is the syllogism: Major premise—God clothes the flowers; Minor premise—people are more important to God than flowers; Conclusion—God can be trusted to provide for these needs. Again, anxiety is needless.

Jesus does not merely discuss the source and folly of the great number of abnormal fears that men possess but he also offers the solution for them, which is not open to successful contradiction. It is a known fact that practicing psychiatrists, psychologists, and counselors are advising these very things to relieve and correct abnormal fears. Such things Jesus taught almost twenty centuries ago in these teachings recorded in the Sermon on the Mount.

But what is the solution to these abnormal fears, and how does it work? Jesus held that the anxious concern of men could be eliminated or redirected through this practice: "Seek ye first the kingdom of God, and his righteousness."

The anxious, neurotic concern of men arises mainly out of an overanxious desire for material things. The solution is, therefore, to subordinate the desire for material things to the desire for spiritual (personal) things. Then, "all these things shall be added unto you."

This does not mean that the solution to neurotic anxiety will only be subjective, wherein the problem will be solved because the things are no longer desired. Rather, it expressly states that with such a personal attitude one will be in a position actually to obtain those material needs.

Seeking God's kingdom and his righteousness redirects both one's thoughts and activities. It moves the center of reference from the self and selfish desires to God and his cause and manner. It is a recentering of personality. The expression "seek ye first" is stated in such a way to mean "go on seeking." Such is not merely an abstract thought process but means the definite habit of seeking.

Psychologically, this is the basis for the defeat of abnormal fear and other neurotic anxieties. Bring the problem out in the open, analyze, and understand it. Often, this alone will banish it. But at any event, abnormal fear can be eliminated with the stronger practice of reconditioning the personality by the development of a new goal outside the self. Broadus' *Commentary* helpfully says, "Our Lord does not simply command us to avoid worldly anxiety, but gives us something positive to do instead, as a means of precluding it." [9]

Holman feels that the main reason for so many abnormal fears is too much self-concern. Should one be successful in turning his thoughts and activities outward, toward the good of others, his neurotic fears and anxieties would vanish.

We need a great cause to which we can commit ourselves, so utter, so commanding, so profoundly worthwhile as to call forth all our loyalty and devotion and make us forget our petty selfish ends. Such a cause religion offers in its ideal of the Kingdom of God, a Kingdom of love and righteousness and the one who is caught by it and gives himself to it sublimates his fears.[10]

All through the passage, Jesus is emphasizing that one should settle his dependence on God to preclude and correct abnormal fears. This is creative faith. Creative faith is stronger than abnormal fear. Acts of creative faith have corrective value. Faith in God is the opposite of abnormal fear.

This emphasis has been well embellished by Peale in his book *Faith Is the Answer*. In this book Peale joins with Blanton, a physician and a psychiatrist. Among other things, they show the matter of fear in its proper light. In regard to faith as the solution to abnormal fear, they have this to say:

The man who believes absolutely in God, in the Divine reliability and goodness, does not hold himself mentally and spiritually rigid, . . . but, on the contrary, rests in complete confidence that all things work together for good to them who believe in God. As a result, he has peace in his mind and quietness at the center of his life. He becomes neither panicky, nor discouraged, for he knows that God watches over him.

This relaxed and peaceful state of mind gives him a clear brain, makes possible the free exercise of all his faculties. Thus he is able to attack his problems with every ounce of ability he possesses.[11]

Fear of Fear

Some people have a fear of fear. They borrow tomorrow's anxieties and bring them over into today's experience. This creates a fear complex—an abnormal reaction akin to a phobia. Jesus recognized that the anxieties of each day's experience are enough for that day without looking ahead for tomorrow's problems and anxieties. Listen as he speaks: "Do not be anxious about tomorrow, for tomorrow will be anxious for itself. Let the day's own trouble be sufficient for the day" (Matt. 6:34, RSV).

Anxiety that is restricted to the day in which it arises can be successfully defeated. Since each day has its unique trials, they may be mastered if handled one at the time and day by day as they arise.

The vast majority of imagined fears never come to pass. The fear complex, with its lack of trust in God, often creates problems that are nonexistent. It causes anxiety neurosis. One lady was worrying because she could not remember what she needed to worry about on a particular day. The creation of new problems adds to the burdens already in existence. It makes one's load heavier than he can bear; hence, the body rebels with fear symptoms. Thus, the anxiety neurosis, popularly called the nervous breakdown, arises.

Though these problems have no objective validity, they are nonetheless real to the person having such irrational fears. They must be met with action that unmasks them. One must come face to face with the real, personal problems which have caused his fears.

This symbolic anxiety also may be met with creative faith. Such faith redirects the personality from the self and its selfishness to a center of reference outside the self. Again, the ideal is "the kingdom of God and his righteousness." This is Jesus' plan for defeating neurotic anxiety. No one has ever offered a more successful program for the prevention of, and release from, abnormal fear.

6

Avoid Negative Habit Hazards

Judge not, that ye be not judged. For with what judgment ye judge, ye shall be judged: and with what measure ye mete, it shall be measured unto you. And why beholdest thou the mote that is in thy brother's eye, but considerest not the beam that is in thine own eye? Or how wilt thou say to thy brother, Let me cast out the mote out of thine eye; and lo, the beam is in thine own eye? Thou hypocrite, cast out first the beam out of thine own eye; and then shalt thou see clearly to cast out the mote out of thy brother's eye.

Give not that which is holy unto the dogs, neither cast your pearls before the swine, lest haply they trample them under their feet, and turn and rend you.

Ask, and it shall be given you; seek, and ye shall find; knock, and it shall be opened unto you: for every one that asketh receiveth, and he that seeketh findeth; and to him that knocketh it shall be opened. Or what man is there of you, who, if his son shall ask him for a loaf, will give him a stone; or if he shall ask for a fish, will give him a serpent? If ye then, being evil, know how to give good gifts unto your children, how much more shall your Father who is in heaven give good things to them that ask him? All things therefore whatsoever ye would that men should do unto you, even so do ye also unto them: for this is the law and the prophets.

Enter ye in by the narrow gate: for wide is the gate, and broad is the way, that leadeth to destruction, and many are they that enter in thereby. For narrow is the gate, and straitened the way, that leadeth unto life, and few are they that find it.

Beware of false prophets, who come to you in sheep's clothing, but inwardly are ravening wolves. By their fruits ye shall know them. Do *men* gather grapes of thorns, or figs of thistles? Even so every good tree bringeth forth good fruit; but the corrupt tree bringeth forth evil fruit. A good tree cannot bring forth evil fruit, neither can a corrupt tree bring forth good fruit. Every tree that bringeth not forth good fruit is hewn down, and cast into the fire. Therefore by their fruits ye shall know them. Not every one that saith unto me, Lord, Lord, shall enter into the kingdom of heaven; but he that doeth the will of my Father who is in heaven. Many will say to me in that day, Lord, Lord, did we not prophesy by thy name, and by thy name cast out demons, and by thy name do many mighty works? And then will I profess unto them, I never knew you: depart from me, ye that work iniquity (Matt. 7:1-23, ASV).

LIVING IS more than a theory. It is a practical reality. We are confronted daily by living issues and by problems which are not merely theoretical. The process of living involves certain hazards which may reduce the substance of living to mere existence.

Jesus was primarily practical in his contacts and teachings. He saw around him every type of human being—the bigot, the humble, the self-righteous, the great, the mediocre, the rich, the poor.

On every hand were to be found the various classes of maladjusted and unhappy people. Their unhappiness was caused largely by their failure to clearly discern or properly evaluate the circumstances or the things behind their discontent.

It was evident to Jesus that there are certain hazards which hinder both effective judgment and effective living. To know and understand these habit hazards is to be forearmed with a defense against them.

Faultfinding

A primary hindrance to sound judgment arises from fault-finding. In psychological terminology this is called projection. Projection is a twofold psychological concept. On the one hand, it consists of thrusting upon others one's ideas or feelings; on the other, it consists of accusing others of the very things of which one is guilty himself.

Present-day writers nearly altogether refer to the last described process as projection. Because of this fact, projection has an almost sinister meaning today.

Since it is frequently unconscious, as well as conscious and deliberate, such an expression of projection is a real hazard to personal understanding and judgment. When unconscious projection occurs, some other person is regarded as being the source of the difficulty. The fact remains that the person doing the faultfinding is actually at fault.

Projection is clearly the outward expression of the inner man. Many people regard projection as normal. To some extent, it is the connection between one's internal and external environment.

Yet, projection is a method to release symbolically some repressed, unwanted idea or attitude. It is thrust outward into a situation or toward another person. Some parents unknowingly project upon their children their own secret ambitions. Often parents try to live their lives again in their children. This kind of projection, too, may frequently include faultfinding.

Projection often appears under the guise of prejudice. One social or racial group accuses the other of hateful practices. All prejudice and faultfinding is an expression of some insecurity, whether it is recognized as such or not.

Young points to projection as a variable device. He says:

It occurs in the development of the delusions of persecution so frequently seen in prejudice and mob behavior, which are similar to the delusions found in the paranoiac patients in our mental hospitals. Projection is often evident in the public behavior of the agitator or intense reformer who foists upon his followers his own secret or private resentment against authority or some institution which he dislikes.[1]

Usually the purpose of projection is to divert attention from the faultfinder to another. It is thus a defense technique which attempts to remove the pressure of moral judgment from one person to another. Projection does not actually pass judgment on the rightness or wrongness of the matter projected. It is an attempt to evade personal responsibility by blaming it on others.

Stolz describes projection with an incident in the lives of two people he called Helen and Walter. They were college students who were in love. During the summer months they were separated by quite some distance. Their only contact was through correspondence, but they constantly wrote of their love for each other.

When Helen and Walter returned to college in the fall, their attitudes at first seemed unchanged. But on their first date a quarrel broke out. Neither could understand why. Apparently, Helen was determined to find fault with Walter. She accused him of unfaithfulness. Though he denied the charges, she became all the more emphatic. She insisted that he had been having an affair with another girl during the summer and charged him with disloyalty. Stolz concludes: "What Helen masked from herself, as well as from Walter, was that it was not he but she who had been carrying on a flirtation. Helen had been flirting just enough to hurt her conscience and to induce the defense reaction of projection."[2]

Jesus recognized the hazard of projection when he said, "Judge not, that ye be not judged." This statement can be understood properly only if its psychological emphasis is given. If there is any reference to a final judgment at the consummation of the age contained herein, it is purely secondary. The primary thing involved in this section on judging has to do with a faultfinding, censorious attitude, and how that attitude is self-defeating to a person's own judgment.

This teaching does not have anything to do with having an opinion contrary to others. It does not suggest that one should refrain from taking a position against someone he knows to be in the wrong for fear that he will be judging.

The emphasis here is on the habit of judging or faultfinding. It does not say "do not ever judge," but it does say, "do not always be judging." The expression in the original language points to habitual action. It means that the habit of constant faultfinding should be avoided. The habit of judging leads to the faultfinding spirit. This is the seed for sinister judging. How difficult it is to have satisfactory relations with self or others when everybody is wrong except you!

This law of getting paid back is an inflexible one. One who judges will receive that same basis of judgment from his fellow man. A person who is severe against others will naturally excite severity against himself.

No one respects a gossiper. Those who engage in gossip have distrust and disrespect for those with whom they gossip. Now gossip is a form of projection. It is practiced, either consciously or unconsciously, by one because of a sense of inferiority. It is an attempt to compensate for this sense of inferiority by trying to reduce another to a position lower than the gossiper subconsciously feels he holds.

It is easy for the critical man to see the mote or speck that is in another's eye, and to overlook the beam or log in his own eye. He is so busy trying to compensate for his inferiority that he cannot, or will not, recognize his trouble as being his own. He insists that his problem has its basis in the other fellow.

Some years ago a teacher had a tremendous inferiority complex. He felt none of his fellow teachers ever did anything worthwhile. The school administrators were grossly incompetent. Everybody was wrong except this teacher. He bitterly talked about the faults of any acquaintance when that person was not present. In a short while it became apparent that this practice was sheer projection. It was not very long before regard for the opinion of this teacher was practically nil.

The bitter man sees his own faults in others and he finds fault constantly. This faultfinding attitude is in itself a glaring fault. It is more offensive than whatever fault is being criticized, even if the fault in the other person has a real basis. The mote of some fault is like a speck as compared with the beam or log of faultfinding. Something of this idea is seen in Miller's caustic statement: "A glaring fault is a capital qualification for seeing faults in others. . . . The proud condemn the proud; the selfish, the selfish. . . . So long as one slings mud he is not annoyed by his own filth." [3]

The habit of seeing faults in others is hazardous to personal judgment. Faultfinding blinds personal vision. Not only does one fail to see the problems of others, though he thinks he does, but he cannot see his own problem clearly. Since he does not know what his real problem is, he cannot correct it.

An end product of projection is paranoia. Often the victim of paranoia suffers from delusions of persecution which have no objective basis.

At a clinical demonstration before a group of college students recently, a psychiatrist presented a patient who was suffering from delusions of persecution. On every matter, except why he was in the state hospital, he seemed very rational. When asked about why he thought he was in the state hospital, he stoutly insisted that he had been framed by the county judge and others. He even suggested the possibility that the Federal Bureau of Investigation was involved. This man determined to get even when he got out of the institution. The psychiatrist said that there was absolutely no objective evidence for his delusions of persecution, but that he was projecting his desires on others. It was further said that the man had vowed to commit murder upon his release from the hospital.

Projection has been known to be the vehicle of one suffering from what has been called reformatory paranoia. This is the very extreme of projection. One who emphasizes some wrong far out of proportion to the need may be projecting some secret sin of his own. When, in an attempt to correct it, some error or wrong is magnified far out of proportion to the attention the thing merits, it then becomes a personality problem to the reformer. When this is true, it is fairly certain that projection is a defense mechanism to distract attention from one's own desire by such fierce attacks on others.

If one would see clearly and fairly, he must rid himself of the beam of faultfinding. He can then see his problem clearly; and, if he really wants to help his brother, he can see clearly how to do it.

When one is free from the spirit of faultfinding, it is possible for him to remove motes from the eyes of others. The passage does not say that one should never try to remove such motes. It does say, however, that such is impossible so long as one has a personal problem as big as faultfinding.

One who is severe in his judgment cannot be of aid because he cannot command the respect of others. Few people, if any, have ever been won from error by being denounced. It is the nature of bitterness to cause the attacked to draw into his shell. Bitterness puts one on his guard and causes him to cling to his error in defense of it. If men are sincere in their desire to cast out motes from others, it must be done through some method other than faultfinding.

The psychological significance upon our judgment in the entire section on faultfinding is related by Miller. He sees a fundamental principle of common sense involved here. Where you do not indulge in the habit of judging others, the result in your own life will be such that you will not come into judgment. To refuse to sit in judgment upon others leaves the critical function free to use its power upon one's self. By constant use of self-criticism, continuous self-discipline inevitably develops. As Miller says, "He who is employed in discerning and denouncing the faults of others will not see his own. He who regards his own will have no spirit to be severe on others." [4]

Familiarity

The other side of faultfinding is too much familiarity. This practice of "fuzzy thinking" is also a hazard to personal judgment and discernment. Jesus counsels men: "Neither cast ye your pearls before the swine."

Much familiarity leads to looseness in thinking and conduct. It destroys mature judgment and clear vision. Some things cannot be shared with everyone. For one to share personal experiences with another who is totally unable to appreciate them is to give that which is holy to dogs and to cast pearls before the swine.

One who has not had a similar experience or thought to

the one which is being shared may be totally unable to have a proper regard for it. He may use that very "pearl" as a basis for a personal attack upon you. Often, one who has not had a genuine religious experience cannot possibly have a basis for the proper appreciation and evaluation of another's experience. Therefore, it means to him what pearls mean to swine.

Similarly, a good thought ought not to be shared with one who cannot understand and appreciate it. In the Talmud a good thought is often called a pearl. Such sharing with an unfit person will often bring scorn and debasement. It will have the effect of marring the very meaning of the experience or thought. Someone has well said that God does not bestow his finest gifts where there is no appropriate response.

Things which are sacred or precious—experiences, thoughts, standards—must be protected from attacks that would try to reduce them to absurdity. To do this, one must be on guard to discern what may be shared, and with what people.

The contrast between faultfinding and familiarity is evident. On the one hand, one is told not to judge critically; on the other hand, he is told to judge fairly and discriminately.

Way to Avoid Extremes

Jesus was not one to offer empty advice. He knew it was a problem to maintain balance between faultfinding and familiarity. Therefore, he offered a method by which one could maintain that balance. This method is contained in his threefold suggestion: ask, seek, knock. To remove these words from their setting and merely make them a general teaching on prayer is to do violence to the context. This destroys much of their psychological significance.

Jesus regards prayer as placing one in the relationship with God that a father and son occupy. His two examples of fatherly provision for the need of a child, bread and fish, reflect that a wise, loving parent will provide a child's needs, though he may not provide all his wants. In this way, but more so, God will provide for all the needs of sound judgment which his child may have.

There is no suggestion of doubt in Jesus' thinking. He regards this as done when one asks, seeks, and knocks. As a father will not scorn his son's reasonable request for needs with something useless or hurtful, God, the Heavenly Father, stands ever ready to supply the needs of his children without upbraiding them.

Jesus' method of prayer removes it from the realm of hit and miss efforts at prayer. More than crisis-experience, prayer is demanded if one would find understanding. The present, imperative tenses of the verbs ask, seek, and knock insist that one exercise the practice habitually—that he go on again and again asking, seeking, and knocking. This is mature prayer, and mature prayer will correct the hazard to understanding, as well as other things.

Mature prayer is both a preventative and a sustaining force. Through this kind of habitual prayer, life may be lifted to higher levels. This involves the use of spiritual preparedness to move from impromptu prayer to disciplined prayer. As Johnson says: "Instead of praying on the impulse of a mood, one may employ prayer to prevent distraction and come to difficult situations resourcefully." [5]

The goal for balance, as well as conduct, is for one to do unto others as he desires them to do unto him. The Golden Rule defines the basis for proper action. One should pray habitually for balance. But one must also do unto others as he would have them do unto him. It is significant that Jesus' emphasis is positive. He says that one should take the initiative and do for others the very things he himself desires, not merely to refrain from doing to another that which he would not want done to himself.

Psychologically, this is the emphasis of the Golden Rule. What you want from others, give that to them. You may not expect to receive from others what you would not give. The Golden Rule is a psychological necessity. It is in the positive application of the Golden Rule that one may discern how to avoid a bitter or thoughtless spirit. What one desires is a safe basis for knowing the treatment and substance of the desires of others.

Fast Living

The good life is made insecure by the broad life. While an open mind and a tentative point of view are aids to personal judgment, the narrow gate is the opening that leads to effective living.

It is almost a paradox that narrow, simple living develops stable lives. Simple foods are the best for the body. Unsophisticated living is best for human personality.

The glitter of the broad way of fast living is very deceptive. It deludes men with the notion that it offers real living, but in reality it leads to destruction. The broad way is so deceptive that it seems the wise thing to follow, "and many there be which go in thereat."

On the other hand, the narrow gate and straitened way do not seem glamorous. They seem so commonplace that by many they are regarded with contempt. Only a few, therefore, find the way that leads to life and effective living.

The emphasis Jesus is making deals with abundant living as a present reality. It is a kind of living that makes for contentment and security now. To hold this teaching to refer to finding life in another world is to do grave injustice to sound interpretation. If such an emphasis is involved at all, it is purely secondary, because "the way" is a term suggesting a manner of living now.

That the narrowed life is best for men is proved by the fact that the many are unadjusted and unhappy. Public and private hospitals are overcrowded with victims of the broad life of fast living. Yet, these represent only a few of unnumbered millions who are suffering the same results.

The force of this truth is clearly recognized by many serious psychologists today. So this teaching is no longer a subject for the preacher only. The broad life has been confronted by the practical tests of effective living. What the broad life does to effective living is all too clear. Its harm to human personality is frightening.

Those who would find life must discipline themselves into the narrow life. No life is effective and meaningful that has not been narrowed. There must be purpose and motive if there is to be effective living. Such does not come from the broad life.

It is as Miller says in discussing the narrowed life: "A life must be narrowed if it is to be effective. Our energies must be focused if they are to be forceful. . . . The focusing power must arise from within. . . . The life must be narrowed by an inner motive." [6]

False Leaders

False teachers are false leaders. They are also a hazard to effective living. The idea that the personality of the teacher does not enter into the total impression of the learner will not bear a close look. It is utterly absurd to minimize the personality of the teacher in the teaching situation.

Price in *Jesus the Teacher* points out that the most important element in the qualification of any teacher is what he is himself. It is still true that one example is worth a thousand words. "What you are thunders so loud I cannot hear what you say."

Furthermore, Price continues, "the best binding for the Gospels is not morocco, but human skin." President Garfield, describing his idea of a university said, "Give me a log hut, with only a simple bench, Mark Hopkins on one end and I on the other." As Price says, "Truth incarnate is the only spiritual truth that makes an effective appeal." Hence, every teacher must feel that his most effective lesson is himself. "This is so because truth is caught more than taught. Unconscious influence is more effective than conscious." [7]

Jesus said, "Beware of false prophets." They appear to be other than they really are. They seek to delude and lead astray. They come in the appearance of gentle, innocent sheep but their real nature is utterly different. They are really like wolves. They come to inflict themselves and their greediness upon others.

The false prophet or teacher does not present himself as himself but rather comes in the name of another. He does not claim to speak for himself. He claims to be speaking upon the authority of another, frequently, God. His utter deception is calculated to rob others of something to satisfy the false teacher's greediness for power, ambition, or money, and to impoverish the other lives.

False teachers are not infallible. A thinking person is not fooled for long. He learns that "by their fruits ye shall know them." The sure way of recognizing false teachers is by their fruits. How do they live? Since their appearance and claims are no proof of their true characters, their sincerity has to be determined by the results, i.e., the products of their teachings.

Trees bear fruit according to their nature. A good tree brings forth good fruit, a corrupt tree cannot bring forth good fruits. It is impossible for a tree to bear fruit that is contrary to its constitution and nature.

One who is not at peace with himself cannot successfully teach others to be so, no matter how long and loud his teachings may be. There is a correspondence between the external product and the internal character of a person.

To help one avoid this pitfall to effective living, Jesus advised that one can know these false prophets by the kind of lives they produce. By their lives, one may know in full both the true and the false teachers.

The false prophet or teacher adds nothing of permanent value to effective living. He offers no lasting values. Therefore, his work is destroyed. That which is useless dies. "By their fruits ye shall know them."

The practical test of fruits or results has definite meaning for personal conduct, likewise. Though religion may be accepted for its ideals and institutions, the more important consideration is how does it work? What effect does it have on conduct?

A man's conduct is ordinarily his voluntary behavior. In ethics one is responsible for what he can control by conscious choice. This has been called the meeting point of religion and ethics. Where one has good motives, he is likely to produce good works.

Johnson asks, "How shall we know that behavior is religious?" He finds two answers. One is the test of action. "By their fruits ye shall know them." It looks toward the results to see what the effects are. These cannot be ignored since almost every kind of a deed—murder, theft, prostitution—has been done in the name of religion. The other test is one's motives. By their motives you shall know them. No act really means much apart from the motive which produced it. As Johnson says:

No act is meaningful until the motive is comprehended. Deeds of service may be grudgingly given under compulsion of slavery, or shrewdly offered for economic gain, or cleverly displayed for political power. In contrast to these, religious service is loving devotion to God offered freely in outgoing concern for other persons.[8]

It seems evident that the test of fruits ultimately tests both motives and acts. No motive or end can be understood apart from its ultimate fruit. While the motive may be hidden for a time, ultimately it must stand the test of fruits also. Jesus included both motives and acts in his teaching on fruit inspection.

False Profession

Finally, false profession is a hazard to effective living. It is not lip service but decisive action that counts in the development of personality. As Jesus said, "Not every one that saith unto me, Lord, Lord, shall enter into the kingdom of heaven; but he that doeth the will of my Father who is in heaven."

Lip service is a subtle form of self-deception. Saying "Lord" is often an attempt to substitute sentimental admiration for heroic conduct. It is a form of alibi that hinders one from continuing to do the will of God.

The alibi is not limited in its application to lip service. It attaches to certain actions as well. Many claim credit for their rationalized actions as being godly in service. They think they are prophesying and casting out demons in God's name.

The psychological concept of rationalization is that reasons other than the real one are given as an alibi for a thought or action. The reason given is but a smoke screen for the real intentions and impulses. Often he who seeks to disguise does so unconsciously. His action is nonetheless a rationalized delusion. In describing the development of such a mechanism of rationalization, Stolz observes: "Sometimes rationalizing as a form of defense thinking begins as downright intellectual dishonesty, but through frequent repetition it assumes validity in the mind of the self-deceived individual. Furthermore, as we have done the questionable we proceed to defend it. What we wish were true may be supposed to be true." [9] If one tells a lie enough times, he begins to believe it himself.

Barry has seen clearly the psychological emphasis in his statement, "It is impossible, as our Lord pointed out in one of his most devastating sayings, for even the most sincere and unselfish of us to be wholly deceived about our own motives." [10]

Our alibis are so false they cause us to make false claims. One thing is certain. No man can accurately count his goods. He who is humble will invariably underestimate his good deeds. The question to be answered is, why do some feel it necessary to brag about their good deeds and many mighty works? Such a claim arises from an unrecognized guilt for not being sincere and doing some good works. Very likely, those who claim credit for many mighty works make a false claim.

This fact remains: it is the self that has been served rather than God. Hence, the many mighty works are just rationalizations. As a matter of fact, they amount to nothing more than ego weapons. Such alibis are tools of false profession.

There is never at any time any personal relationship existing between the false professor and God. This is obvious from Jesus' statement, "Then will I profess unto them, I never [at any time] knew you: depart from me, ye that work iniquity." False profession defeats a personal relationship with God. Such profession is a tremendous hazard to effective living.

Negative habit hazards defeat one in his quest for the happy, stable, secure life. Whether it be faultfinding, familiarity, fast living, false prophets, or false profession, all such negative habits should be shunned. These destroy security in living, and Jesus wanted them avoided.

7

Discover Life's Real Security

Every one therefore that heareth these words of mine, and doeth them, shall be likened unto a wise man, who built his house upon the rock: and the rain descended, and the floods came, and the winds blew, and beat upon that house; and it fell not: for it was founded upon the rock. And every one that heareth these words of mine, and doeth them not, shall be likened unto a foolish man, who built his house upon the sand: and the rain descended, and the floods came, and the winds blew, and smote upon that house; and it fell: and great was the fall thereof (Matt. 7:24–27, ASV).

THE PLAIN of Sharon is reported to have clay of a very inferior kind. Not only are the earthenware jars made from it often worthless but also its building bricks offer little resistance to the weather. Houses built out of brick made from this clay are not very substantial or lasting.

This fact was very much in the general knowledge of the people of Jesus' day. On the Day of Atonement even the high priest offered a special prayer, asking the Lord to grant that their houses might not become their tombs.

The figure used by Jesus of two builders was one which was designed to have real meaning to his audience. Probably most of them knew the condition of the clay and sand in the Plain of Sharon. A great many knew of the building practices employed there. On these plains, it was a frequent practice of the imprudent to build on sand. The prayers of the high priest attest to the fact that many houses had doubtless been demolished by the wind and by the water which was carried down from the mountains to these plains. Evidence reveals that the country in the plains below the mountains sometimes has torrent beds more than a half mile in width. These plains are dry in the summer and present a level of waste sand and stones.

Here are two builders. The one builds on the sand in these torrent beds, for the land is easy to obtain. He may even use the stones that have collected in this area after previous storms. This builder just does not think through the matter to the possible consequences. When the storms and the rains cascade down, as they are certain to do, the house of this builder will be destroyed, for it is built on an insecure foundation.

The other builder is thoughtful. He considers the matter of the foundation. He builds his house upon the rock; and when the winds and rain come, it falls not. His wisdom is justified, for he has considered not merely the abstract possibilities, but rather what likely will happen every year, and is most certain to happen now and then. The wisdom here is not exceptional, just a display of ordinary common sense.

These two builders graphically depict the difference in secure and insecure bases for building a life. As men build their lives, they, no doubt, will use one or the other of two foundations—the unsubstantial or the substantial.

The unsubstantial foundation on which to build a life is that of materialism. It appears to be sound, but fundamentally it is as insecure as sand. It is, in its very nature, transient and temporal.

The substantial foundation on which to build a life is that of spiritual, personal law. It is fundamental, lasting, and secure. This spiritual law is not a surface consideration, as materialism is; therefore, some prudence is required in laying hold of it.

A secure life is not the product of haphazard planning. Such a life does not just happen. It requires some understanding and thoughtfulness of means and ends. Physical development may produce growth in the physical body. But in the area of human personality, lives do not develop properly apart from a secure plan or foundation for living. Growing up is the usual law of the physical; spiritual law is the order of growth and development in the sphere of human personality.

Jesus knew the secret of the spiritual law. He knew that his teachings were the fundamental spiritual truths of the universe. For one to live in harmony with them is to build a strong, secure life. For one to live in utter disregard or in apathy to them is to invite insecurity and unhappiness.

To the criticism that there are people who apparently build secure lives without recognizing Jesus, or being Christian, it has been said that these people accept Jesus' teaching whether they intend to do so or not. They may not accept his person, but they either consciously or unconsciously live by his teachings.

The thoughtful man faces the facts of life and lives in harmony with them. The foolish man either disregards or refuses to face the facts of life. One is like the wise man who considered the sand, the winds, and the water. The other man failed to take them into consideration.

Either men give consideration to the spiritual, personal laws of the universe or they fail or refuse to consider them. When men have regard for these spiritual laws, they both hear and do them. If men fail or refuse to have regard for the fundamental spiritual law, they may hear it, but they do not practice it. They fail to adjust and discipline themselves to this fundamental spiritual law.

One thing is significant however. When men fail to take a positive relationship to the fundamental spiritual law, they are not exempt from the consequences of such failure. No more are they exempt than they would be if they failed to give consideration to physical law.

Gravity will help a man if he uses it. When he uses it, he can build a wall straight. When he builds in opposition to gravity, it is out of plumb. The same is true of human beings. Those who build their lives in keeping with personality-producing laws which are grounded in spiritual truth build upon a secure foundation. To build the life out of harmony with them is to build on the insecurity of sand.

The superstructure above the foundation may appear to be very satisfactory, but the foundation will determine its real worth. Many acts of social service may appear to be philanthropical when actually they are expressions of selfishness. The testing time comes for every attitude and act, and that which is not founded on spiritual fundamentals meets destruction.

Mental assent to the spiritual law is not a sufficient foundation for life. There must be the element of putting one's assent into action. One may hear and understand, and yet not *do* the spiritual law. A person does not actually align himself with a thing unless he positively accepts the thing by consistent action. A common fallacy among men is the thought that they can assent mentally to the spiritual laws but fail to put them into practice and yet build a strong life on such a foundation. What foolishness!

Jesus' teachings must be accepted in mind, in feeling, and in action. One cannot merely accept them intellectually. They are not too idealistic to be put into practice. Yet, a vast number of people, even Christians, live as though his teachings for the secure life are not relevant.

What happens to a man psychologically when he hears without heeding? Impression without proper expression leads to depression. This makes a weak foundation for personality. If one does not act on a vital spiritual impression, he is likely to repress it into the subconscious. But if one does react to an impression positively, he may develop a stronger personality. To react positively helps develop the habit of healthy reaction. It is made easier to react positively with each succeeding positive reaction.

Now the man who regards himself as a Christian but does not know what Jesus taught is fooling himself. Should he know Jesus' teachings but fail to act on them, he still does not build upon that secure foundation.

Assent must be put into practice to really learn the content of a thing as well as to establish a secure foundation for psychological development. One only learns those things he does. If one would really learn, he must do as well as hear.

Security or insecurity is largely psychological. To a big extent, individual ideas create one or the other for us. What is security to one person is not necessarily security to another. Some think that security in living depends upon how much money or credit one has. Jesus taught otherwise. History's most secure person, Jesus, claimed ownership of nothing at all. Anyone who thinks Jesus was insecure, unstable, neurotic, or psychotic is in need of psychiatric help.

Insecurity has many faces. It wears many masks. People try to hide it under fear, bitterness, sickness, fighting, delinquency, prejudice, hate, even work.

A well-known multimillionaire became ill with anxiety over an expense of $150. Why should a man worth several million dollars feel so much anxiety over such a small amount? No amount of money can by itself make anyone secure or insecure.

A friend relates this experience: It seems that a friend of his was determined to make a lot of money, no matter what it cost. When he first started in business, he rented store space in a very busy part of town. During the first dozen or so years, he and his wife slept, ate, and lived in the rear of the store. The living area was separated from the rest of the store by a curtain. He was always on hand for a customer, day or night.

He seemed reasonably happy, but the desire to make a lot of money kept gnawing away. In time he made money. Then the desire for money turned to a desire for things—houses, cars, properties. At last, he bought a mansion. Then came the servants, several cars of the sixteen-cylinder makes, several large bank accounts. He had arrived, he thought.

But for him, his security soon became insecurity. The servants feared him, his family detested him, and his wife refused to speak to him. This man had reached his pinnacle of success. He had everything he had worked for but actually nothing which made him happy. His own words reveal his empty life: "I am the most miserable man alive." Alive? Or had he become a physically functioning, psychological corpse? Do you suppose his need all along the way was to think upon the words of Jesus, "Blessed are the meek," or the self-controlled? Yes, he that hears "these words of mine" and does not do them shall be likened to the foolish man that built his house upon the sand.

Political power is sometimes thought to be a source of security. But the King of kings, to the dismay of many in his day, refused to exercise any political power. Yet he himself said, "All power is given unto me in heaven and in earth." The anxiety and insecurity created by the struggle to obtain or retain political power make it evident that political power and security are not the same.

Few men have felt more insecure in their political position than Herod. It was he who issued the decree for the slaughter of infants when he who was to be king of the Jews was born. But this was only one of a series of murders committed by Herod in his attempt to retain his political power. How insecure he must have been. For fear of losing his kingdom, he even had his beautiful wife Mariamne put to death.

But what about political power in the "little kingdoms"? What about the little kingdoms in business, society, and similar areas? Men strive to secure for themselves some artificial power through position, prestige, educational status. And they do it to be served rather than to serve.

Smith worked for a plant with many of the usual titles current in the business world today. There was a supervisor for everything from filling ink wells to emptying them. Smith made up his mind he must have one of these little kingdoms, regardless of what principles he had to sacrifice. Moreover, anyone in his way to the top had to be removed. But it must be done subtly. Company interests must appear the important thing.

Like other businesses, alcohol at social functions had become a symbol of success with Smith's organization. Now Smith did not especially care for alcohol, but he identified it with success. So he learned to serve it in his home for business reasons. He never drank in the absence of others. However, he felt it necessary to serve drinks at business and social gatherings.

How does Smith's conduct reveal personal insecurity? It is necessary to know a bit more about him. For years Smith had worked as a clerk in a large office. The work was routine, at times boring. No chance to be very creative was possible.

And he had reached the top of the ladder in his job. Then suddenly an opportunity for a defense plant job came. The new job offered challenge and a chance to be creative, to use his imagination. Also it opened up the way to several little kingdoms.

Alcohol was identified with success in the new environment. So it became first an unconscious and then a conscious symbol of success. A mask of insecurity? You bet! It became such a complete mask that Smith regarded it as essential to getting ahead, and he has the ulcers to prove it. The lust for a little kingdom is an insecure foundation of blow sand. Why not hear and do the words of Jesus "Blessed are the poor in spirit"?

Another mask of insecurity is seen in the instalment-buying craze. We will buy almost anything on easy monthly payments. Nothing down and twenty-four to thirty-six months to pay is the password of the day to the world of gadgets and gimmicks. Of course, it finally works out, nothing down and forever paying.

Most people have had the delusion of easy payments. To have "things" has too often become one's economic, as well as psychological, insecurity. Tensions and fears result. Many people are earning more than ever, yet have more debt. Everything or everyone except self is blamed. At times men are tempted to blame this problem on the Almighty. Their hunger and thirst for things can never be satisfied. Lives built on these hungers are insecure, and they create other insecurities. Lives built on a hunger and thirst for righteousness are on a more secure foundation. It makes one more secure to be right and to do right.

Anger and bitterness are often masks of insecurity. Take the teen-ager who is a rebel without reason. The question to be answered is not why is he angry or bitter. The question is what is the anger or bitterness a cover up for? Why is it needed? It must be serving some purpose, or he would give it up.

A group of boys walking on the sidewalk toward town met two women of another race. As they approached, one of the boys drew up his fist and hit one of the women in the face. Now they had not said nor done anything to provoke this attack.

What was this boy trying to prove and to whom? Not a word among the boys had been said about the approaching women. Was he trying to show off? Maybe, but more likely he was taking out his inner civil war anger. He was bitter with himself and this was his way of showing it. Was he any stronger or more secure after striking the woman? Certainly not! All he succeeded in doing was to display a basic insecurity which he felt a need to protect. More than anything else, to his shifting sands foundation he needed to apply Jesus' words, "Blessed are the peacemakers."

All delinquency may be nothing more than conduct reducible to some kind of insecurity. Insecurity brought on by the need to give or receive love may mask itself in many symbols. Over the long pull, it is possible to spark in others either bitterness or love, for either may be learned from others. When a person feels unwanted or rejected for a long period of time, he is likely to build a protective house for his insecurity. But he may build it with materials of the same kind.

Some think the greatest single cause of insecurity is rejection, disapproval, lack of love. Most people can stand an empty stomach easier than an empty heart. But they come nearer to getting love and approval when they give love and approval. Security in living has a sure foundation in hearing and heeding Jesus' words, "Love your enemies, and pray for them that persecute you."

Still another mask of insecurity displays its ugly face in the struggle for social status. Again, why does one feel a need to lord it over others? The day of titles of nobility is passing fast. But many other devices are at hand. Not the least of these is words. A class struggle continues over the use of "proper" and "improper" words. If one uses proper words, he belongs to a higher social group, especially if he can look down on the fellow who uses improper words. Really now, why all the fury over words? Is this a sensible basis for one to have contempt for others? A study of word changes through the years should cure this insecurity.

Yes, anything which causes bad relations with self or others masks some kind of insecurity. Otherwise, why does one feel it necessary to harp on it? To lessen social insecurity, Jesus said, "Whatsoever ye would that men should do unto you, even so do ye also unto them." Can you top it?

Security consists in finding satisfaction for one's physical and psychological needs. This is secured by regular use of Jesus' principles contained in the Sermon on the Mount. This practice also helps one to see the difference between his needs and his wants.

To have security one needs to understand himself. Jesus spoke of those things in the Beatitudes that help this understanding. Security in this area means hearing and heeding.

There are social needs also. The main one is social maturity. To grow up socially requires one to turn from childishness and his point of view to see the other fellow and his point of view. This is both hearing and heeding.

Personal security depends also upon spiritual adjustment. Camouflage must be removed, and vital connection with God must be made. Giving, praying, and fasting solely to God harvests this aspect of security.

A life free from excessive anxiety tends to be more secure.

Hearing and heeding Jesus' teaching of eliminating anxiety through practical acts of trust gives great strength. The trust becomes practical when one seeks first "his kingdom, and his righteousness." Is there a better way to defeat anxiety than constantly to put God first?

Security grows by avoiding those things which give one a negative outlook. Faultfinding, familiarity, fast living, false teachers, and false profession make people less secure. To replace them with positive habits is hearing and heeding Jesus' teaching. More security spreads into the life built on this part of Jesus' foundation.

In Jesus' parable it has been pointed out that the foolish builder's folly was not his deliberately choosing a bad foundation. It was in his failing to give any consideration to the matter of foundation. He began to build haphazardly without regard to the foundation. His choice not to give regard is just as much a choice as the deliberate selection of a poor foundation. After all, every act of a free moral being is a choice, even though the choice consists in letting someone else do his choosing. The lack of bad intent on the part of the foolish cannot lessen the consequences of a poor choice. The error of the foolish builder was in his not thinking. Though his choice was not one of conscious selection, he chose to be inconsiderate. Whatever consequences naturally result from it will of necessity be his. The spiritual law is also fully binding in this respect.

As a house built on an insecure foundation will not withstand the physical storms and stresses, so also a life built on an insecure foundation will not stand under the storms and stresses to which human personality is subjected. Some people survive because they are fortunate enough to be spared the rains and floods and winds.

Only those with a secure foundation can withstand the

trials of life. In most instances the insecure cannot withstand the normal stresses of living without some personality
breakdown. It may be that the only difference in breakdown
of those who have built a life on an insecure basis is in the
amount. It may merely resolve itself to a question of how
much.

The matter of the extent of destruction of the life founded
on an insecure basis is shown in the words of Jesus "and
great was the fall thereof." The idea of utter and complete
ruin is contained herein. The destruction of the life built on
some basis other than the spiritual, personal laws of the universe is thorough and complete. Storms and floods are calculated to demolish completely the house which has an insecure foundation. Trials and problems are calculated to
demolish completely a life which has not been built on the
positive, personal acceptance of Jesus' spiritual teachings.

The secure life, however, has been founded on the rock.
It is stable and lasting. The expression "was founded" uses
the Greek tense called the pluperfect passive. It is one of the
very few uses of this tense in the New Testament. Depicted
is an abiding condition of something completed in the past.
This rock foundation is the secure spiritual, personal law. It
abides as a secure foundation, because it remains secure.

It is evident that the primary thing emphasized is secure
and insecure living as a present or a here and now reality.
Of course, a secure foundation has survival value unto eter-
nity. But Jesus' first concern was to cause men to recognize,
and positively accept, the spiritual interpretation of life.
Then they should put it into practice in their daily living.
Those who would hear and heed Jesus' teachings have already begun building on a secure foundation.

The secure life is the one that takes Jesus seriously. It gives
regard to his words and builds upon them by acting in ac-

cordance with the teaching. This person hears discerningly and continues to put the teaching into practice in his personal life. As Miller says, "The secret of security is to hear the words of Jesus and do them. . . . If I give myself to accomplish His purposes, my security is as sure as His victory. My life is founded upon a rock." [1]

One discovers life's real security through accepting and living by Jesus' teachings as though his very life depended upon such action, for indeed it really does.

Notes

Chapter 2

1. Alexander Balmain Bruce, *The Synoptic Gospels* (*The Expositor's Greek Testament*, ed. W. Robertson Nicoll [Grand Rapids: Wm. B. Eerdmans Publishing Co., n.d.]), I, 98.

2. Archibald Thomas Robertson, *Word Pictures in the New Testament* (Nashville: Broadman Press, 1930), I, 41.

3. R. C. H. Lenski, *The Interpretation of Matthew* (Columbus: Wartburg Press, 1933), p. 197.

4. Adam Clarke, *Matthew* (*Commentary on the Entire Bible* [New York: Abingdon Press, 1940]), V, 67.

5. Rollo May, *The Art of Counseling* (New York: Abingdon Press, 1939), p. 166.

6. Clarke, *op. cit.*, p. 25.

Chapter 3

1. Robertson, *op. cit.*, p. 45.

2. F. R. Barry, *Christianity and Psychology* (New York: George H. Doran Co., 1925), p, 102.

3. Joshua Loth Liebman, *Peace of Mind* (New York: Simon and Schuster, Inc., 1946), p. 26.

4. Leslie D. Weatherhead, *Psychology and Life* (New York: Abingdon Press, 1935), p. 112.

5. Clarke, *op. cit.*, p. 74.

6. John A. Broadus, *Matthew* (*An American Commentary on the New Testament*, ed. Alvah Hovey [Philadelphia: American Baptist Publication Society, n.d.]), I, 120.

7. Clarke, *op. cit.*, p. 77.

Chapter 4

1. Arthur Carr, *The Gospel According to St. Matthew* (*Cambridge Greek Testament for Schools and Colleges*, ed. J. J. S.

Perowne [Cambridge: Cambridge University Press, 1896]), p. 127.

2. Bruce, *op. cit.*, p. 117.

3. *Ibid.*

4. Clarke, *op. cit.*, p. 84.

5. Karl R. Stolz, *Pastoral Psychology* (New York: Abingdon-Cokesbury Press, 1932), p. 223.

6. William Douglas Chamberlain, *The Manner of Prayer* (Philadelphia: Westminster Press, 1943), pp. 19 ff.

7. Clarke, *op. cit.*, pp. 87–88.

8. James H. Snowden, *The Psychology of Religion* (New York: Fleming H. Revell Co., 1916), p. 237.

Chapter 5

1. Paul E. Johnson, *Psychology of Religion* (New York: Abingdon Press, 1959), p. 74. Used by permission.

2. Lenski, *op. cit.*, p. 275.

3. Bruce, *op. cit.*, p. 123.

4. Weatherhead, *op. cit.*, p. 174.

5. Lenski, *op. cit.*, p. 280.

6. Barry, *op. cit.*, p. 35.

7. Clarke, op. cit., p. 91.

8. Robertson, *op. cit.*, p. 59.

9. Broadus, *op. cit.*, p. 151.

10. Charles T. Holman, *The Religion of a Healthy Mind* (New York: Round Table Press, Inc., 1939), p. 52.

11. Norman Vincent Peale and Smiley Blanton, *Faith Is the Answer* (3rd ed.; Englewood Cliffs, N.J.: Prentice-Hall, Inc., 1955), p. 78.

Chapter 6

1. Kimball Young, *Personality and the Problems of Adjustment* (2d. ed.; New York: Appleton-Century-Crofts, Inc., 1946), p. 118.

2. Stolz, *op. cit.*, p. 181.

3. Robert Henry Miller, *The Life Portrayed in the Sermon on the Mount* (Boston: W. A. Wilde Co., 1934), pp. 161–63.

4. *Ibid.*, p. 155.

5. Johnson, *op. cit.*, p. 136.

6. Miller, *op. cit.*, p. 183.

7. J. M. Price, *Jesus the Teacher* (Nashville: Broadman Press, 1946), pp. 1–2.

8. Johnson, *op. cit.*, p. 213.

9. Stolz, *op. cit.*, p. 182.

10. Barry, *op. cit.*, p. 34.

Chapter 7

1. Miller, *op. cit.*, pp. 214–15.

Bibliography

BARRY, F. R. *Christianity and Psychology.* New York: George H. Doran Co., 1925.

BOWMAN, JOHN WICK, and TAPP, ROLAND W. *The Gospel from the Mount.* Philadelphia: Westminster Press, 1957.

BROADUS, JOHN A. *Matthew.* (*An American Commentary on the New Testament,* ed. ALVAH HOVEY, Vol. I.) Philadelphia: American Baptist Publication Society, n.d.

BRUCE, ALEXANDER BALMAIN. *The Synoptic Gospels.* (*The Expositor's Greek Testament,* ed. W. ROBERTSON NICOLL, Vol. I.) Grand Rapids: William B. Eerdmans Publishing Co., n.d.

BUTTRICK, GEORGE A. (ed.). *Matthew.* (*The Interpreter's Bible,* Vol. VII.) New York: Abingdon Press, 1951.

CARR, ARTHUR. *The Gospel According to St. Matthew.* (*Cambridge Greek Testament for Schools and Colleges,* ed. J. J. S. PEROWNE.) Cambridge: Cambridge University Press, 1896.

CHAMBERLAIN, WILLIAM DOUGLAS. *The Manner of Prayer.* Philadelphia: Westminster Press, 1943.

CLARKE, ADAM. *Matthew.* (*Commentary on the Entire Bible,* Vol. V.) New York: Abingdon Press, 1940.

CONNICK, C. MILO. *Build on the Rock: You and the Sermon on the Mount.* Westwood: Fleming H. Revell Co., 1960.

HOLMAN, CHARLES T. *The Religion of a Healthy Mind.* New York: Round Table Press, Inc., 1939.

JOHNSON, PAUL E. *Psychology of Religion.* New York: Abingdon Press, 1959.

LENSKI, R. C. H. *The Interpretation of Matthew.* Columbus: Wartburg Press, 1933.

LIEBMAN, JOSHUA LOTH. *Peace of Mind.* New York: Simon and Schuster, Inc., 1946.

MAY, ROLLO. *The Art of Counseling*. New York: Abingdon Press, 1939.

MILLER, ROBERT HENRY. *The Life Portrayed in the Sermon on the Mount*. Boston: W. A. Wilde Co., 1934.

PEALE, NORMAN VINCENT. *A Guide to Confident Living*. New York: Prentice-Hall, Inc., 1948.

PEALE, NORMAN VINCENT, and BLANTON, SMILEY. *Faith Is the Answer*. 3rd ed.; Englewood Cliffs, N.J.: Prentice-Hall, Inc., 1955.

PRICE, J. M. *Jesus the Teacher*. Nashville: Broadman Press, 1946.

ROBERTSON, ARCHIBALD THOMAS. *Word Pictures in the New Testament*. Vol. I. Nashville: Broadman Press, 1930.

SNOWDEN, JAMES H. *The Psychology of Religion*. New York: Fleming H. Revell Co., 1916.

STOLZ, KARL R. *Pastoral Psychology*. New York: Abingdon-Cokesbury Press, 1932.

WEATHERHEAD, LESLIE D. *Psychology and Life*. New York: Abingdon Press, 1935.

WILLIAMSON, ROBERT L. *Effective Public Prayer*. Nashville: Broadman Press, 1960.

YOUNG, KIMBALL. *Personality and the Problems of Adjustment*. 2d. ed.; New York: Appleton-Century-Crofts, Inc., 1946.

Scripture Index